C-1118   CAREER EXAMINATION SERIES

This is your
PASSBOOK for...

Assistant Teacher

Test Preparation Study Guide
Questions & Answers

NATIONAL LEARNING CORPORATION®

COPYRIGHT NOTICE

This book is SOLELY intended for, is sold ONLY to, and its use is RESTRICTED to individual, bona fide applicants or candidates who qualify by virtue of having seriously filed applications for appropriate license, certificate, professional and/or promotional advancement, higher school matriculation, scholarship, or other legitimate requirements of education and/or governmental authorities.

This book is NOT intended for use, class instruction, tutoring, training, duplication, copying, reprinting, excerption, or adaptation, etc., by:

1) Other publishers
2) Proprietors and/or Instructors of "Coaching" and/or Preparatory Courses
3) Personnel and/or Training Divisions of commercial, industrial, and governmental organizations
4) Schools, colleges, or universities and/or their departments and staffs, including teachers and other personnel
5) Testing Agencies or Bureaus
6) Study groups which seek by the purchase of a single volume to copy and/or duplicate and/or adapt this material for use by the group as a whole without having purchased individual volumes for each of the members of the group
7) Et al.

Such persons would be in violation of appropriate Federal and State statutes.

PROVISION OF LICENSING AGREEMENTS – Recognized educational, commercial, industrial, and governmental institutions and organizations, and others legitimately engaged in educational pursuits, including training, testing, and measurement activities, may address request for a licensing agreement to the copyright owners, who will determine whether, and under what conditions, including fees and charges, the materials in this book may be used them. In other words, a licensing facility exists for the legitimate use of the material in this book on other than an individual basis. However, it is asseverated and affirmed here that the material in this book CANNOT be used without the receipt of the express permission of such a licensing agreement from the Publishers. Inquiries re licensing should be addressed to the company, attention rights and permissions department.

All rights reserved, including the right of reproduction in whole or in part, in any form or by any means, electronic or mechanical, including photocopying, recording, or by any information storage and retrieval system, without permission in writing from the Publisher.

Copyright © 2025 by
National Learning Corporation

212 Michael Drive, Syosset, NY 11791
(516) 921-8888 • www.passbooks.com
E-mail: info@passbooks.com

PASSBOOK® SERIES

THE *PASSBOOK® SERIES* has been created to prepare applicants and candidates for the ultimate academic battlefield – the examination room.

At some time in our lives, each and every one of us may be required to take an examination – for validation, matriculation, admission, qualification, registration, certification, or licensure.

Based on the assumption that every applicant or candidate has met the basic formal educational standards, has taken the required number of courses, and read the necessary texts, the *PASSBOOK® SERIES* furnishes the one special preparation which may assure passing with confidence, instead of failing with insecurity. Examination questions – together with answers – are furnished as the basic vehicle for study so that the mysteries of the examination and its compounding difficulties may be eliminated or diminished by a sure method.

This book is meant to help you pass your examination provided that you qualify and are serious in your objective.

The entire field is reviewed through the huge store of content information which is succinctly presented through a provocative and challenging approach – the question-and-answer method.

A climate of success is established by furnishing the correct answers at the end of each test.

You soon learn to recognize types of questions, forms of questions, and patterns of questioning. You may even begin to anticipate expected outcomes.

You perceive that many questions are repeated or adapted so that you can gain acute insights, which may enable you to score many sure points.

You learn how to confront new questions, or types of questions, and to attack them confidently and work out the correct answers.

You note objectives and emphases, and recognize pitfalls and dangers, so that you may make positive educational adjustments.

Moreover, you are kept fully informed in relation to new concepts, methods, practices, and directions in the field.

You discover that you are actually taking the examination all the time: you are preparing for the examination by "taking" an examination, not by reading extraneous and/or supererogatory textbooks.

In short, this PASSBOOK®, used directedly, should be an important factor in helping you to pass your test.

ASSISTANT TEACHER

DUTIES
Assists teachers in a paraprofessional capacity with students in a classroom and school facilities to facilitate learning and teaching objectives.

SCOPE OF THE EXAMINATION
The written test will cover knowledge, skills and/or abilities in such areas as:
1. Principles and practices of education and learning;
2. Verbal abilities;
3. Reading comprehension; and
4. Basic mathematical ability.

HOW TO TAKE A TEST

I. YOU MUST PASS AN EXAMINATION

A. *WHAT EVERY CANDIDATE SHOULD KNOW*

Examination applicants often ask us for help in preparing for the written test. What can I study in advance? What kinds of questions will be asked? How will the test be given? How will the papers be graded?

As an applicant for a civil service examination, you may be wondering about some of these things. Our purpose here is to suggest effective methods of advance study and to describe civil service examinations.

Your chances for success on this examination can be increased if you know how to prepare. Those "pre-examination jitters" can be reduced if you know what to expect. You can even experience an adventure in good citizenship if you know why civil service exams are given.

B. *WHY ARE CIVIL SERVICE EXAMINATIONS GIVEN?*

Civil service examinations are important to you in two ways. As a citizen, you want public jobs filled by employees who know how to do their work. As a job seeker, you want a fair chance to compete for that job on an equal footing with other candidates. The best-known means of accomplishing this two-fold goal is the competitive examination.

Exams are widely publicized throughout the nation. They may be administered for jobs in federal, state, city, municipal, town or village governments or agencies.

Any citizen may apply, with some limitations, such as the age or residence of applicants. Your experience and education may be reviewed to see whether you meet the requirements for the particular examination. When these requirements exist, they are reasonable and applied consistently to all applicants. Thus, a competitive examination may cause you some uneasiness now, but it is your privilege and safeguard.

C. *HOW ARE CIVIL SERVICE EXAMS DEVELOPED?*

Examinations are carefully written by trained technicians who are specialists in the field known as "psychological measurement," in consultation with recognized authorities in the field of work that the test will cover. These experts recommend the subject matter areas or skills to be tested; only those knowledges or skills important to your success on the job are included. The most reliable books and source materials available are used as references. Together, the experts and technicians judge the difficulty level of the questions.

Test technicians know how to phrase questions so that the problem is clearly stated. Their ethics do not permit "trick" or "catch" questions. Questions may have been tried out on sample groups, or subjected to statistical analysis, to determine their usefulness.

Written tests are often used in combination with performance tests, ratings of training and experience, and oral interviews. All of these measures combine to form the best-known means of finding the right person for the right job.

II. HOW TO PASS THE WRITTEN TEST

A. NATURE OF THE EXAMINATION

To prepare intelligently for civil service examinations, you should know how they differ from school examinations you have taken. In school you were assigned certain definite pages to read or subjects to cover. The examination questions were quite detailed and usually emphasized memory. Civil service exams, on the other hand, try to discover your present ability to perform the duties of a position, plus your potentiality to learn these duties. In other words, a civil service exam attempts to predict how successful you will be. Questions cover such a broad area that they cannot be as minute and detailed as school exam questions.

In the public service similar kinds of work, or positions, are grouped together in one "class." This process is known as *position-classification*. All the positions in a class are paid according to the salary range for that class. One class title covers all of these positions, and they are all tested by the same examination.

B. FOUR BASIC STEPS

1) Study the announcement

How, then, can you know what subjects to study? Our best answer is: "Learn as much as possible about the class of positions for which you've applied." The exam will test the knowledge, skills and abilities needed to do the work.

Your most valuable source of information about the position you want is the official exam announcement. This announcement lists the training and experience qualifications. Check these standards and apply only if you come reasonably close to meeting them.

The brief description of the position in the examination announcement offers some clues to the subjects which will be tested. Think about the job itself. Review the duties in your mind. Can you perform them, or are there some in which you are rusty? Fill in the blank spots in your preparation.

Many jurisdictions preview the written test in the exam announcement by including a section called "Knowledge and Abilities Required," "Scope of the Examination," or some similar heading. Here you will find out specifically what fields will be tested.

2) Review your own background

Once you learn in general what the position is all about, and what you need to know to do the work, ask yourself which subjects you already know fairly well and which need improvement. You may wonder whether to concentrate on improving your strong areas or on building some background in your fields of weakness. When the announcement has specified "some knowledge" or "considerable knowledge," or has used adjectives like "beginning principles of…" or "advanced … methods," you can get a clue as to the number and difficulty of questions to be asked in any given field. More questions, and hence broader coverage, would be included for those subjects which are more important in the work. Now weigh your strengths and weaknesses against the job requirements and prepare accordingly.

3) Determine the level of the position

Another way to tell how intensively you should prepare is to understand the level of the job for which you are applying. Is it the entering level? In other words, is this the position in which beginners in a field of work are hired? Or is it an intermediate or advanced level? Sometimes this is indicated by such words as "Junior" or "Senior" in the class title. Other jurisdictions use Roman numerals to designate the level – Clerk I, Clerk II, for example. The word "Supervisor" sometimes appears in the title. If the level is not indicated by the title, check the description of duties. Will you be working under very close supervision, or will you have responsibility for independent decisions in this work?

4) Choose appropriate study materials

Now that you know the subjects to be examined and the relative amount of each subject to be covered, you can choose suitable study materials. For beginning level jobs, or even advanced ones, if you have a pronounced weakness in some aspect of your training, read a modern, standard textbook in that field. Be sure it is up to date and has general coverage. Such books are normally available at your library, and the librarian will be glad to help you locate one. For entry-level positions, questions of appropriate difficulty are chosen – neither highly advanced questions, nor those too simple. Such questions require careful thought but not advanced training.

If the position for which you are applying is technical or advanced, you will read more advanced, specialized material. If you are already familiar with the basic principles of your field, elementary textbooks would waste your time. Concentrate on advanced textbooks and technical periodicals. Think through the concepts and review difficult problems in your field.

These are all general sources. You can get more ideas on your own initiative, following these leads. For example, training manuals and publications of the government agency which employs workers in your field can be useful, particularly for technical and professional positions. A letter or visit to the government department involved may result in more specific study suggestions, and certainly will provide you with a more definite idea of the exact nature of the position you are seeking.

III. KINDS OF TESTS

Tests are used for purposes other than measuring knowledge and ability to perform specified duties. For some positions, it is equally important to test ability to make adjustments to new situations or to profit from training. In others, basic mental abilities not dependent on information are essential. Questions which test these things may not appear as pertinent to the duties of the position as those which test for knowledge and information. Yet they are often highly important parts of a fair examination. For very general questions, it is almost impossible to help you direct your study efforts. What we can do is to point out some of the more common of these general abilities needed in public service positions and describe some typical questions.

1) General information

Broad, general information has been found useful for predicting job success in some kinds of work. This is tested in a variety of ways, from vocabulary lists to questions about current events. Basic background in some field of work, such as sociology or economics, may be sampled in a group of questions. Often these are principles which have become familiar to most persons through exposure rather than through formal training. It is difficult to advise you how to study for these questions; being alert to the world around you is our best suggestion.

2) Verbal ability

An example of an ability needed in many positions is verbal or language ability. Verbal ability is, in brief, the ability to use and understand words. Vocabulary and grammar tests are typical measures of this ability. Reading comprehension or paragraph interpretation questions are common in many kinds of civil service tests. You are given a paragraph of written material and asked to find its central meaning.

3) Numerical ability

Number skills can be tested by the familiar arithmetic problem, by checking paired lists of numbers to see which are alike and which are different, or by interpreting charts and graphs. In the latter test, a graph may be printed in the test booklet which you are asked to use as the basis for answering questions.

4) Observation

A popular test for law-enforcement positions is the observation test. A picture is shown to you for several minutes, then taken away. Questions about the picture test your ability to observe both details and larger elements.

5) Following directions

In many positions in the public service, the employee must be able to carry out written instructions dependably and accurately. You may be given a chart with several columns, each column listing a variety of information. The questions require you to carry out directions involving the information given in the chart.

6) Skills and aptitudes

Performance tests effectively measure some manual skills and aptitudes. When the skill is one in which you are trained, such as typing or shorthand, you can practice. These tests are often very much like those given in business school or high school courses. For many of the other skills and aptitudes, however, no short-time preparation can be made. Skills and abilities natural to you or that you have developed throughout your lifetime are being tested.

Many of the general questions just described provide all the data needed to answer the questions and ask you to use your reasoning ability to find the answers. Your best preparation for these tests, as well as for tests of facts and ideas, is to be at your physical and mental best. You, no doubt, have your own methods of getting into an exam-taking mood and keeping "in shape." The next section lists some ideas on this subject.

IV. KINDS OF QUESTIONS

Only rarely is the "essay" question, which you answer in narrative form, used in civil service tests. Civil service tests are usually of the short-answer type. Full instructions for answering these questions will be given to you at the examination. But in case this is your first experience with short-answer questions and separate answer sheets, here is what you need to know:

1) **Multiple-choice Questions**

Most popular of the short-answer questions is the "multiple choice" or "best answer" question. It can be used, for example, to test for factual knowledge, ability to solve problems or judgment in meeting situations found at work.

A multiple-choice question is normally one of three types—
- It can begin with an incomplete statement followed by several possible endings. You are to find the one ending which *best* completes the statement, although some of the others may not be entirely wrong.
- It can also be a complete statement in the form of a question which is answered by choosing one of the statements listed.

- It can be in the form of a problem – again you select the best answer.

Here is an example of a multiple-choice question with a discussion which should give you some clues as to the method for choosing the right answer:

When an employee has a complaint about his assignment, the action which will *best* help him overcome his difficulty is to
- A. discuss his difficulty with his coworkers
- B. take the problem to the head of the organization
- C. take the problem to the person who gave him the assignment
- D. say nothing to anyone about his complaint

In answering this question, you should study each of the choices to find which is best. Consider choice "A" – Certainly an employee may discuss his complaint with fellow employees, but no change or improvement can result, and the complaint remains unresolved. Choice "B" is a poor choice since the head of the organization probably does not know what assignment you have been given, and taking your problem to him is known as "going over the head" of the supervisor. The supervisor, or person who made the assignment, is the person who can clarify it or correct any injustice. Choice "C" is, therefore, correct. To say nothing, as in choice "D," is unwise. Supervisors have and interest in knowing the problems employees are facing, and the employee is seeking a solution to his problem.

2) True/False Questions

The "true/false" or "right/wrong" form of question is sometimes used. Here a complete statement is given. Your job is to decide whether the statement is right or wrong.

SAMPLE: A roaming cell-phone call to a nearby city costs less than a non-roaming call to a distant city.

This statement is wrong, or false, since roaming calls are more expensive.

This is not a complete list of all possible question forms, although most of the others are variations of these common types. You will always get complete directions for answering questions. Be sure you understand *how* to mark your answers – ask questions until you do.

V. RECORDING YOUR ANSWERS

Computer terminals are used more and more today for many different kinds of exams.

For an examination with very few applicants, you may be told to record your answers in the test booklet itself. Separate answer sheets are much more common. If this separate answer sheet is to be scored by machine – and this is often the case – it is highly important that you mark your answers correctly in order to get credit.

An electronic scoring machine is often used in civil service offices because of the speed with which papers can be scored. Machine-scored answer sheets must be marked with a pencil, which will be given to you. This pencil has a high graphite content which responds to the electronic scoring machine. As a matter of fact, stray dots may register as answers, so do not let your pencil rest on the answer sheet while you are pondering the correct answer. Also, if your pencil lead breaks or is otherwise defective, ask for another.

Since the answer sheet will be dropped in a slot in the scoring machine, be careful not to bend the corners or get the paper crumpled.

The answer sheet normally has five vertical columns of numbers, with 30 numbers to a column. These numbers correspond to the question numbers in your test booklet. After each number, going across the page are four or five pairs of dotted lines. These short dotted lines have small letters or numbers above them. The first two pairs may also have a "T" or "F" above the letters. This indicates that the first two pairs only are to be used if the questions are of the true-false type. If the questions are multiple choice, disregard the "T" and "F" and pay attention only to the small letters or numbers.

Answer your questions in the manner of the sample that follows:

32. The largest city in the United States is
    A. Washington, D.C.
    B. New York City
    C. Chicago
    D. Detroit
    E. San Francisco

1) Choose the answer you think is best. (New York City is the largest, so "B" is correct.)
2) Find the row of dotted lines numbered the same as the question you are answering. (Find row number 32)
3) Find the pair of dotted lines corresponding to the answer. (Find the pair of lines under the mark "B.")
4) Make a solid black mark between the dotted lines.

VI. BEFORE THE TEST

Common sense will help you find procedures to follow to get ready for an examination. Too many of us, however, overlook these sensible measures. Indeed, nervousness and fatigue have been found to be the most serious reasons why applicants fail to do their best on civil service tests. Here is a list of reminders:

- Begin your preparation early – Don't wait until the last minute to go scurrying around for books and materials or to find out what the position is all about.
- Prepare continuously – An hour a night for a week is better than an all-night cram session. This has been definitely established. What is more, a night a week for a month will return better dividends than crowding your study into a shorter period of time.
- Locate the place of the exam – You have been sent a notice telling you when and where to report for the examination. If the location is in a different town or otherwise unfamiliar to you, it would be well to inquire the best route and learn something about the building.
- Relax the night before the test – Allow your mind to rest. Do not study at all that night. Plan some mild recreation or diversion; then go to bed early and get a good night's sleep.
- Get up early enough to make a leisurely trip to the place for the test – This way unforeseen events, traffic snarls, unfamiliar buildings, etc. will not upset you.
- Dress comfortably – A written test is not a fashion show. You will be known by number and not by name, so wear something comfortable.

- Leave excess paraphernalia at home – Shopping bags and odd bundles will get in your way. You need bring only the items mentioned in the official notice you received; usually everything you need is provided. Do not bring reference books to the exam. They will only confuse those last minutes and be taken away from you when in the test room.
- Arrive somewhat ahead of time – If because of transportation schedules you must get there very early, bring a newspaper or magazine to take your mind off yourself while waiting.
- Locate the examination room – When you have found the proper room, you will be directed to the seat or part of the room where you will sit. Sometimes you are given a sheet of instructions to read while you are waiting. Do not fill out any forms until you are told to do so; just read them and be prepared.
- Relax and prepare to listen to the instructions
- If you have any physical problem that may keep you from doing your best, be sure to tell the test administrator. If you are sick or in poor health, you really cannot do your best on the exam. You can come back and take the test some other time.

VII. AT THE TEST

The day of the test is here and you have the test booklet in your hand. The temptation to get going is very strong. Caution! There is more to success than knowing the right answers. You must know how to identify your papers and understand variations in the type of short-answer question used in this particular examination. Follow these suggestions for maximum results from your efforts:

1) Cooperate with the monitor

The test administrator has a duty to create a situation in which you can be as much at ease as possible. He will give instructions, tell you when to begin, check to see that you are marking your answer sheet correctly, and so on. He is not there to guard you, although he will see that your competitors do not take unfair advantage. He wants to help you do your best.

2) Listen to all instructions

Don't jump the gun! Wait until you understand all directions. In most civil service tests you get more time than you need to answer the questions. So don't be in a hurry. Read each word of instructions until you clearly understand the meaning. Study the examples, listen to all announcements and follow directions. Ask questions if you do not understand what to do.

3) Identify your papers

Civil service exams are usually identified by number only. You will be assigned a number; you must not put your name on your test papers. Be sure to copy your number correctly. Since more than one exam may be given, copy your exact examination title.

4) Plan your time

Unless you are told that a test is a "speed" or "rate of work" test, speed itself is usually not important. Time enough to answer all the questions will be provided, but this does not mean that you have all day. An overall time limit has been set. Divide the total time (in minutes) by the number of questions to determine the approximate time you have for each question.

5) **Do not linger over difficult questions**

If you come across a difficult question, mark it with a paper clip (useful to have along) and come back to it when you have been through the booklet. One caution if you do this – be sure to skip a number on your answer sheet as well. Check often to be sure that you have not lost your place and that you are marking in the row numbered the same as the question you are answering.

6) **Read the questions**

Be sure you know what the question asks! Many capable people are unsuccessful because they failed to *read* the questions correctly.

7) **Answer all questions**

Unless you have been instructed that a penalty will be deducted for incorrect answers, it is better to guess than to omit a question.

8) **Speed tests**

It is often better NOT to guess on speed tests. It has been found that on timed tests people are tempted to spend the last few seconds before time is called in marking answers at random – without even reading them – in the hope of picking up a few extra points. To discourage this practice, the instructions may warn you that your score will be "corrected" for guessing. That is, a penalty will be applied. The incorrect answers will be deducted from the correct ones, or some other penalty formula will be used.

9) **Review your answers**

If you finish before time is called, go back to the questions you guessed or omitted to give them further thought. Review other answers if you have time.

10) **Return your test materials**

If you are ready to leave before others have finished or time is called, take ALL your materials to the monitor and leave quietly. Never take any test material with you. The monitor can discover whose papers are not complete, and taking a test booklet may be grounds for disqualification.

VIII. EXAMINATION TECHNIQUES

1) Read the general instructions carefully. These are usually printed on the first page of the exam booklet. As a rule, these instructions refer to the timing of the examination; the fact that you should not start work until the signal and must stop work at a signal, etc. If there are any *special* instructions, such as a choice of questions to be answered, make sure that you note this instruction carefully.

2) When you are ready to start work on the examination, that is as soon as the signal has been given, read the instructions to each question booklet, underline any key words or phrases, such as *least, best, outline, describe* and the like. In this way you will tend to answer as requested rather than discover on reviewing your paper that you *listed without describing*, that you selected the *worst* choice rather than the *best* choice, etc.

3) If the examination is of the objective or multiple-choice type – that is, each question will also give a series of possible answers: A, B, C or D, and you are called upon to select the best answer and write the letter next to that answer on your answer paper – it is advisable to start answering each question in turn. There may be anywhere from 50 to 100 such questions in the three or four hours allotted and you can see how much time would be taken if you read through all the questions before beginning to answer any. Furthermore, if you come across a question or group of questions which you know would be difficult to answer, it would undoubtedly affect your handling of all the other questions.

4) If the examination is of the essay type and contains but a few questions, it is a moot point as to whether you should read all the questions before starting to answer any one. Of course, if you are given a choice – say five out of seven and the like – then it is essential to read all the questions so you can eliminate the two that are most difficult. If, however, you are asked to answer all the questions, there may be danger in trying to answer the easiest one first because you may find that you will spend too much time on it. The best technique is to answer the first question, then proceed to the second, etc.

5) Time your answers. Before the exam begins, write down the time it started, then add the time allowed for the examination and write down the time it must be completed, then divide the time available somewhat as follows:
    - If 3-1/2 hours are allowed, that would be 210 minutes. If you have 80 objective-type questions, that would be an average of 2-1/2 minutes per question. Allow yourself no more than 2 minutes per question, or a total of 160 minutes, which will permit about 50 minutes to review.
    - If for the time allotment of 210 minutes there are 7 essay questions to answer, that would average about 30 minutes a question. Give yourself only 25 minutes per question so that you have about 35 minutes to review.

6) The most important instruction is to *read each question* and make sure you know what is wanted. The second most important instruction is to *time yourself properly* so that you answer every question. The third most important instruction is to *answer every question*. Guess if you have to but include something for each question. Remember that you will receive no credit for a blank and will probably receive some credit if you write something in answer to an essay question. If you guess a letter – say "B" for a multiple-choice question – you may have guessed right. If you leave a blank as an answer to a multiple-choice question, the examiners may respect your feelings but it will not add a point to your score. Some exams may penalize you for wrong answers, so in such cases *only*, you may not want to guess unless you have some basis for your answer.

7) Suggestions
    a. Objective-type questions
        1. Examine the question booklet for proper sequence of pages and questions
        2. Read all instructions carefully
        3. Skip any question which seems too difficult; return to it after all other questions have been answered
        4. Apportion your time properly; do not spend too much time on any single question or group of questions

5. Note and underline key words – *all, most, fewest, least, best, worst, same, opposite,* etc.
6. Pay particular attention to negatives
7. Note unusual option, e.g., unduly long, short, complex, different or similar in content to the body of the question
8. Observe the use of "hedging" words – *probably, may, most likely,* etc.
9. Make sure that your answer is put next to the same number as the question
10. Do not second-guess unless you have good reason to believe the second answer is definitely more correct
11. Cross out original answer if you decide another answer is more accurate; do not erase until you are ready to hand your paper in
12. Answer all questions; guess unless instructed otherwise
13. Leave time for review

b. Essay questions
1. Read each question carefully
2. Determine exactly what is wanted. Underline key words or phrases.
3. Decide on outline or paragraph answer
4. Include many different points and elements unless asked to develop any one or two points or elements
5. Show impartiality by giving pros and cons unless directed to select one side only
6. Make and write down any assumptions you find necessary to answer the questions
7. Watch your English, grammar, punctuation and choice of words
8. Time your answers; don't crowd material

8) Answering the essay question

Most essay questions can be answered by framing the specific response around several key words or ideas. Here are a few such key words or ideas:

M's: manpower, materials, methods, money, management
P's: purpose, program, policy, plan, procedure, practice, problems, pitfalls, personnel, public relations

a. Six basic steps in handling problems:
1. Preliminary plan and background development
2. Collect information, data and facts
3. Analyze and interpret information, data and facts
4. Analyze and develop solutions as well as make recommendations
5. Prepare report and sell recommendations
6. Install recommendations and follow up effectiveness

b. Pitfalls to avoid
1. *Taking things for granted* – A statement of the situation does not necessarily imply that each of the elements is necessarily true; for example, a complaint may be invalid and biased so that all that can be taken for granted is that a complaint has been registered

2. *Considering only one side of a situation* – Wherever possible, indicate several alternatives and then point out the reasons you selected the best one
3. *Failing to indicate follow up* – Whenever your answer indicates action on your part, make certain that you will take proper follow-up action to see how successful your recommendations, procedures or actions turn out to be
4. *Taking too long in answering any single question* – Remember to time your answers properly

IX. AFTER THE TEST

Scoring procedures differ in detail among civil service jurisdictions although the general principles are the same. Whether the papers are hand-scored or graded by machine we have described, they are nearly always graded by number. That is, the person who marks the paper knows only the number – never the name – of the applicant. Not until all the papers have been graded will they be matched with names. If other tests, such as training and experience or oral interview ratings have been given, scores will be combined. Different parts of the examination usually have different weights. For example, the written test might count 60 percent of the final grade, and a rating of training and experience 40 percent. In many jurisdictions, veterans will have a certain number of points added to their grades.

After the final grade has been determined, the names are placed in grade order and an eligible list is established. There are various methods for resolving ties between those who get the same final grade – probably the most common is to place first the name of the person whose application was received first. Job offers are made from the eligible list in the order the names appear on it. You will be notified of your grade and your rank as soon as all these computations have been made. This will be done as rapidly as possible.

People who are found to meet the requirements in the announcement are called "eligibles." Their names are put on a list of eligible candidates. An eligible's chances of getting a job depend on how high he stands on this list and how fast agencies are filling jobs from the list.

When a job is to be filled from a list of eligibles, the agency asks for the names of people on the list of eligibles for that job. When the civil service commission receives this request, it sends to the agency the names of the three people highest on this list. Or, if the job to be filled has specialized requirements, the office sends the agency the names of the top three persons who meet these requirements from the general list.

The appointing officer makes a choice from among the three people whose names were sent to him. If the selected person accepts the appointment, the names of the others are put back on the list to be considered for future openings.

That is the rule in hiring from all kinds of eligible lists, whether they are for typist, carpenter, chemist, or something else. For every vacancy, the appointing officer has his choice of any one of the top three eligibles on the list. This explains why the person whose name is on top of the list sometimes does not get an appointment when some of the persons lower on the list do. If the appointing officer chooses the second or third eligible, the No. 1 eligible does not get a job at once, but stays on the list until he is appointed or the list is terminated.

X. HOW TO PASS THE INTERVIEW TEST

The examination for which you applied requires an oral interview test. You have already taken the written test and you are now being called for the interview test – the final part of the formal examination.

You may think that it is not possible to prepare for an interview test and that there are no procedures to follow during an interview. Our purpose is to point out some things you can do in advance that will help you and some good rules to follow and pitfalls to avoid while you are being interviewed.

What is an interview supposed to test?

The written examination is designed to test the technical knowledge and competence of the candidate; the oral is designed to evaluate intangible qualities, not readily measured otherwise, and to establish a list showing the relative fitness of each candidate – as measured against his competitors – for the position sought. Scoring is not on the basis of "right" and "wrong," but on a sliding scale of values ranging from "not passable" to "outstanding." As a matter of fact, it is possible to achieve a relatively low score without a single "incorrect" answer because of evident weakness in the qualities being measured.

Occasionally, an examination may consist entirely of an oral test – either an individual or a group oral. In such cases, information is sought concerning the technical knowledges and abilities of the candidate, since there has been no written examination for this purpose. More commonly, however, an oral test is used to supplement a written examination.

Who conducts interviews?

The composition of oral boards varies among different jurisdictions. In nearly all, a representative of the personnel department serves as chairman. One of the members of the board may be a representative of the department in which the candidate would work. In some cases, "outside experts" are used, and, frequently, a businessman or some other representative of the general public is asked to serve. Labor and management or other special groups may be represented. The aim is to secure the services of experts in the appropriate field.

However the board is composed, it is a good idea (and not at all improper or unethical) to ascertain in advance of the interview who the members are and what groups they represent. When you are introduced to them, you will have some idea of their backgrounds and interests, and at least you will not stutter and stammer over their names.

What should be done before the interview?

While knowledge about the board members is useful and takes some of the surprise element out of the interview, there is other preparation which is more substantive. It *is* possible to prepare for an oral interview – in several ways:

1) Keep a copy of your application and review it carefully before the interview

This may be the only document before the oral board, and the starting point of the interview. Know what education and experience you have listed there, and the sequence and dates of all of it. Sometimes the board will ask you to review the highlights of your experience for them; you should not have to hem and haw doing it.

2) Study the class specification and the examination announcement

Usually, the oral board has one or both of these to guide them. The qualities, characteristics or knowledges required by the position sought are stated in these documents. They offer valuable clues as to the nature of the oral interview. For example, if the job involves supervisory responsibilities, the announcement will usually indicate that knowledge of modern supervisory methods and the qualifications of the candidate as a supervisor will be tested. If so, you can expect such questions, frequently in the form of a hypothetical situation which you are expected to solve. NEVER go into an oral without knowledge of the duties and responsibilities of the job you seek.

3) Think through each qualification required

Try to visualize the kind of questions you would ask if you were a board member. How well could you answer them? Try especially to appraise your own knowledge and background in each area, *measured against the job sought*, and identify any areas in which you are weak. Be critical and realistic – do not flatter yourself.

4) Do some general reading in areas in which you feel you may be weak

For example, if the job involves supervision and your past experience has NOT, some general reading in supervisory methods and practices, particularly in the field of human relations, might be useful. Do NOT study agency procedures or detailed manuals. The oral board will be testing your understanding and capacity, not your memory.

5) Get a good night's sleep and watch your general health and mental attitude

You will want a clear head at the interview. Take care of a cold or any other minor ailment, and of course, no hangovers.

What should be done on the day of the interview?

Now comes the day of the interview itself. Give yourself plenty of time to get there. Plan to arrive somewhat ahead of the scheduled time, particularly if your appointment is in the fore part of the day. If a previous candidate fails to appear, the board might be ready for you a bit early. By early afternoon an oral board is almost invariably behind schedule if there are many candidates, and you may have to wait. Take along a book or magazine to read, or your application to review, but leave any extraneous material in the waiting room when you go in for your interview. In any event, relax and compose yourself.

The matter of dress is important. The board is forming impressions about you – from your experience, your manners, your attitude, and your appearance. Give your personal appearance careful attention. Dress your best, but not your flashiest. Choose conservative, appropriate clothing, and be sure it is immaculate. This is a business interview, and your appearance should indicate that you regard it as such. Besides, being well groomed and properly dressed will help boost your confidence.

Sooner or later, someone will call your name and escort you into the interview room. *This is it.* From here on you are on your own. It is too late for any more preparation. But remember, you asked for this opportunity to prove your fitness, and you are here because your request was granted.

What happens when you go in?

The usual sequence of events will be as follows: The clerk (who is often the board stenographer) will introduce you to the chairman of the oral board, who will introduce you to the other members of the board. Acknowledge the introductions before you sit down. Do not be surprised if you find a microphone facing you or a stenotypist sitting by. Oral interviews are usually recorded in the event of an appeal or other review.

Usually the chairman of the board will open the interview by reviewing the highlights of your education and work experience from your application – primarily for the benefit of the other members of the board, as well as to get the material into the record. Do not interrupt or comment unless there is an error or significant misinterpretation; if that is the case, do not hesitate. But do not quibble about insignificant matters. Also, he will usually ask you some question about your education, experience or your present job – partly to get you to start talking and to establish the interviewing "rapport." He may start the actual questioning, or turn it over to one of the other members. Frequently, each member undertakes the questioning on a particular area, one in which he is perhaps most competent, so you can expect each member to participate in the examination. Because time is limited, you may also expect some rather abrupt switches in the direction the questioning takes, so do not be upset by it. Normally, a board member will not pursue a single line of questioning unless he discovers a particular strength or weakness.

After each member has participated, the chairman will usually ask whether any member has any further questions, then will ask you if you have anything you wish to add. Unless you are expecting this question, it may floor you. Worse, it may start you off on an extended, extemporaneous speech. The board is not usually seeking more information. The question is principally to offer you a last opportunity to present further qualifications or to indicate that you have nothing to add. So, if you feel that a significant qualification or characteristic has been overlooked, it is proper to point it out in a sentence or so. Do not compliment the board on the thoroughness of their examination – they have been sketchy, and you know it. If you wish, merely say, "No thank you, I have nothing further to add." This is a point where you can "talk yourself out" of a good impression or fail to present an important bit of information. Remember, *you close the interview yourself*.

The chairman will then say, "That is all, Mr. _____, thank you." Do not be startled; the interview is over, and quicker than you think. Thank him, gather your belongings and take your leave. Save your sigh of relief for the other side of the door.

How to put your best foot forward

Throughout this entire process, you may feel that the board individually and collectively is trying to pierce your defenses, seek out your hidden weaknesses and embarrass and confuse you. Actually, this is not true. They are obliged to make an appraisal of your qualifications for the job you are seeking, and they want to see you in your best light. Remember, they must interview all candidates and a non-cooperative candidate may become a failure in spite of their best efforts to bring out his qualifications. Here are 15 suggestions that will help you:

1) **Be natural – Keep your attitude confident, not cocky**

If you are not confident that you can do the job, do not expect the board to be. Do not apologize for your weaknesses, try to bring out your strong points. The board is interested in a positive, not negative, presentation. Cockiness will antagonize any board member and make him wonder if you are covering up a weakness by a false show of strength.

2) **Get comfortable, but don't lounge or sprawl**

Sit erectly but not stiffly. A careless posture may lead the board to conclude that you are careless in other things, or at least that you are not impressed by the importance of the occasion. Either conclusion is natural, even if incorrect. Do not fuss with your clothing, a pencil or an ashtray. Your hands may occasionally be useful to emphasize a point; do not let them become a point of distraction.

3) **Do not wisecrack or make small talk**

This is a serious situation, and your attitude should show that you consider it as such. Further, the time of the board is limited – they do not want to waste it, and neither should you.

4) Do not exaggerate your experience or abilities

In the first place, from information in the application or other interviews and sources, the board may know more about you than you think. Secondly, you probably will not get away with it. An experienced board is rather adept at spotting such a situation, so do not take the chance.

5) If you know a board member, do not make a point of it, yet do not hide it

Certainly you are not fooling him, and probably not the other members of the board. Do not try to take advantage of your acquaintanceship – it will probably do you little good.

6) Do not dominate the interview

Let the board do that. They will give you the clues – do not assume that you have to do all the talking. Realize that the board has a number of questions to ask you, and do not try to take up all the interview time by showing off your extensive knowledge of the answer to the first one.

7) Be attentive

You only have 20 minutes or so, and you should keep your attention at its sharpest throughout. When a member is addressing a problem or question to you, give him your undivided attention. Address your reply principally to him, but do not exclude the other board members.

8) Do not interrupt

A board member may be stating a problem for you to analyze. He will ask you a question when the time comes. Let him state the problem, and wait for the question.

9) Make sure you understand the question

Do not try to answer until you are sure what the question is. If it is not clear, restate it in your own words or ask the board member to clarify it for you. However, do not haggle about minor elements.

10) Reply promptly but not hastily

A common entry on oral board rating sheets is "candidate responded readily," or "candidate hesitated in replies." Respond as promptly and quickly as you can, but do not jump to a hasty, ill-considered answer.

11) Do not be peremptory in your answers

A brief answer is proper – but do not fire your answer back. That is a losing game from your point of view. The board member can probably ask questions much faster than you can answer them.

12) Do not try to create the answer you think the board member wants

He is interested in what kind of mind you have and how it works – not in playing games. Furthermore, he can usually spot this practice and will actually grade you down on it.

13) Do not switch sides in your reply merely to agree with a board member

Frequently, a member will take a contrary position merely to draw you out and to see if you are willing and able to defend your point of view. Do not start a debate, yet do not surrender a good position. If a position is worth taking, it is worth defending.

14) Do not be afraid to admit an error in judgment if you are shown to be wrong
The board knows that you are forced to reply without any opportunity for careful consideration. Your answer may be demonstrably wrong. If so, admit it and get on with the interview.

15) Do not dwell at length on your present job
The opening question may relate to your present assignment. Answer the question but do not go into an extended discussion. You are being examined for a *new* job, not your present one. As a matter of fact, try to phrase ALL your answers in terms of the job for which you are being examined.

Basis of Rating
Probably you will forget most of these "do's" and "don'ts" when you walk into the oral interview room. Even remembering them all will not ensure you a passing grade. Perhaps you did not have the qualifications in the first place. But remembering them will help you to put your best foot forward, without treading on the toes of the board members.

Rumor and popular opinion to the contrary notwithstanding, an oral board wants you to make the best appearance possible. They know you are under pressure – but they also want to see how you respond to it as a guide to what your reaction would be under the pressures of the job you seek. They will be influenced by the degree of poise you display, the personal traits you show and the manner in which you respond.

ABOUT THIS BOOK

This book contains tests divided into Examination Sections. Go through each test, answering every question in the margin. We have also attached a sample answer sheet at the back of the book that can be removed and used. At the end of each test look at the answer key and check your answers. On the ones you got wrong, look at the right answer choice and learn. Do not fill in the answers first. Do not memorize the questions and answers, but understand the answer and principles involved. On your test, the questions will likely be different from the samples. Questions are changed and new ones added. If you understand these past questions you should have success with any changes that arise. Tests may consist of several types of questions. We have additional books on each subject should more study be advisable or necessary for you. Finally, the more you study, the better prepared you will be. This book is intended to be the last thing you study before you walk into the examination room. Prior study of relevant texts is also recommended. NLC publishes some of these in our Fundamental Series. Knowledge and good sense are important factors in passing your exam. Good luck also helps. So now study this Passbook, absorb the material contained within and take that knowledge into the examination. Then do your best to pass that exam.

EXAMINATION SECTION

EXAMINATION SECTION
TEST 1

DIRECTIONS: Each question or incomplete statement is followed by several suggested answers or completions. Select the one that BEST answers the question or completes the statement. *PRINT THE LETTER OF THE CORRECT ANSWER IN THE SPACE AT THE RIGHT.*

1. Which of the following basic listening skills is prerequisite to the others?

    A. Identifying stated main ideas
    B. Making generalizations
    C. Drawing conclusions
    D. Comparing different points of view

2. Which of the following factors is the MOST important indication of a child's readiness for reading?

    A. Motor development
    B. Maturational age
    C. Physical development
    D. Chronological age

Questions 3-4.

DIRECTIONS: Read the passage below from MYTHOLOGY, and then answer Questions 3 and 4.

   The first written record of Greece is the ILIAD. Greek mythology begins with Homer, generally believed to be not earlier than a thousand years before Christ. The ILIAD is, or contains, the oldest Greek literature; and it is written in a rich and subtle and beautiful language which must have had behind it centuries when men were striving to express themselves with clarity and beauty, an indisputable proof of civilization. The tales of Greek mythology do not throw any clear light upon what early mankind was like - a matter, it would seem, of more importance to us, who are their descendants intellectually, artistically, and politically, too. Nothing we learn about them is alien to ourselves.

3. Which line from the passage is a statement of fact?

    A. The tales of Greek mythology do not throw any clear light upon what early mankind was like.
    B. Nothing we learn about them is alien to ourselves.
    C. It is written in a rich and subtle and beautiful language which must have had behind it centuries when men were striving to express themselves with clarity and beauty.
    D. The ILIAD is, or contains, the oldest Greek literature.

4. The author's point of view toward the subject of this passage is one of

    A. humorous indulgence
    B. respect and admiration
    C. tongue-in-cheek flattery
    D. longing and nostalgia

5. Which of the following sentences is capitalized CORRECTLY?

    A. My aunt told Uncle Leon about the documentary she saw at the Biograph Theater.
    B. In the Southern Hemisphere, the first day of winter is in June.

C. The Riveras plan to spend their vacation in California at Yosemite national Park.
D. Gloria's room had an Eastern exposure, and the sun woke her up at dawn.

6. Which sentence demonstrates proper pronoun-antecedent agreement?

   A. The council of officials has announced his decision.
   B. All public parks will close its gates at 5:00 P.M.
   C. All wardens must report to her stations by 5:15 P.M.
   D. Workers in public parks must display their identification cards.

7. Which of the following is a compound sentence?

   A. Sonya painted the sign, and I did the lettering.
   B. Without a dictionary, I couldn't check my spelling.
   C. No one noticed the mistakes until this morning.
   D. Of twelve words on the sign, three were misspelled.

8. What number is represented above?

   A. 136   B. 316   C. 361   D. 631

9. Marcy is practicing for a track meet. Each day she runs around a quarter-mile track two and one-half times. How many miles does she run in five days?
   _____ miles.

   A. 5/8   B. 1 1/4   C. 3 1/8   D. 12 1/2

10. Everything in a hardware store is being sold at 20 percent off the regular price. Mark bought a garden hose regularly priced at $12.95 and a wheelbarrow regularly priced at $23.95.
    What operations are needed to calculate how much Mark had to pay?

    A. Divide 0.20 by $23.95 and add $12.95
    B. Add $12.95 and $23.95 and multiply the sum by 0.8
    C. Multiply $23.95 by 0.20 and add $12.95
    D. Subtract $12.95 from $23.95 and multiply by 0.2

11. How many lines of symmetry does an equilateral triangle have?

    A. One   B. Two   C. Three   D. Four

12. Humans are responsible for the extinction of other species PRIMARILY through

    A. environmental pollution
    B. experimental hybridization
    C. hunting and poaching
    D. habitat destruction

13. Replacement of a cold air mass by a warm air mass is usually FIRST indicated by the formation of which cloud type?

    A. Cirrus
    B. Cumulonimbus
    C. Cumulus
    D. Stratus

14. Edward is writing a brief report on specific examples of extreme weather conditions in the United States. Which of the following pieces of information would be MOST relevant to his report?

    A. A hurricane is defined as a storm in which winds blow at greater than 74 miles per hour near the storm center.
    B. The highest temperature ever recorded was in Libya in 1922; it was 136 degrees Fahrenheit.
    C. In the Texas panhandle, snowfall averages about 2 feet each year.
    D. The greatest rainfall ever recorded in 1 minute was 1.23 inches; it occurred in Unionville, Maryland.

15. In the United States, all citizens have the responsibility to

    A. petition the government
    B. exercise freedom of religion
    C. serve on juries
    D. determine the rate of income tax

16. According to the map above, Bombay, India, is located at APPROXIMATELY which longitude and latitude?
    Longitude _____; latitude _____.

    A. 73° E; 19° N
    B. 21° N; 73° E
    C. 73° E; 21° N
    D. 19° N; 73° E

17. The Monroe Doctrine was intended to
    A. promote commercial relations with the Concert of Europe
    B. protect American sailors from involuntary service
    C. prevent European expansion in Latin America
    D. open the southeastern United States to settlement

18. Which of the following activities would be MOST helpful for a sixth grader in developing his or her individual response to art?
    A. Matching artistic techniques to artworks
    B. Participating in a critique of various artworks
    C. Matching artists to their works
    D. Learning terminology associated with art criticism

KEY (CORRECT ANSWERS)

1.	A	11.	C
2.	B	12.	D
3.	D	13.	A
4.	B	14.	D
5.	A	15.	C
6.	D	16.	A
7.	A	17.	C
8.	B	18.	B
9.	C		
10.	B		

TEST 2

DIRECTIONS: Each question or incomplete statement is followed by several suggested answers or completions. Select the one that BEST answers the question or completes the statement. *PRINT THE LETTER OF THE CORRECT ANSWER IN THE SPACE AT THE RIGHT.*

1. At the early elementary level, which of the following activities would be MOST appropriate for developing fine-motor skills?

    A. Tying shoelaces
    B. Pushing a swing
    C. Throwing a ball
    D. Skipping rope

    1.____

2. When educationally disadvantaged students enter school, the problems they face are MOST often a function of

    A. traumatic childhood incidents
    B. an inability to think clearly in solving problems
    C. overemphasis on achievement
    D. a lack of exposure to positive, varied experiences

    2.____

3. Which of the following criteria is MOST important in determining whether a given learning opportunity is appropriate for an elementary class?

    A. Levels of cognitive and psychomotor development among students
    B. Content of available textbooks
    C. Usefulness of the subject matter in life outside the classroom
    D. Testing programs in use at the school

    3.____

4. Which of the following is MOST important for a teacher to consider when selecting materials for a specific lesson?

    A. Relationship to learner objectives
    B. Popularity of the material
    C. Relationship to the teacher's personal interests
    D. Publisher of the material

    4.____

5. Recent data from nationwide standardized tests show that students in the Alpha school district scored below average in mathematics skills.
Based on these data, which is the MOST appropriate short-term goal for this school district?

    A. Emphasize higher-level skills in mathematics
    B. Assess students' strengths and weaknesses in reading
    C. Improve Alpha's curriculum in reading and mathematics
    D. Compare the Alpha curriculum with those of other districts

    5.____

6. A class has just read *Jack and the Beanstalk*.
Which of the following questions would be MOST appropriate for a teacher to ask if the objective of the lesson is to teach interpretive reading skills?

    A. How many times did Jack climb the beanstalk?
    B. Who planted the beanstalk?

    6.____

5

C. What did Jack do before he climbed the beanstalk?
D. Why did Jack climb the beanstalk the third time?

7. In the scope and sequence of social studies skills, the emphasis of objectives in the elementary grades tends to follow a progression from

   A. history to politics
   B. self to family to community
   C. culture to economics
   D. world to nation to neighborhood

7.____

8. A teacher notes that on a particular multiple-choice test item, about the same number of students chose each of the four responses.
This MOST likely means that the

   A. item was too easy for the students
   B. students did not follow the directions
   C. item had two correct responses
   D. students were guessing at the answer

8.____

9. One advantage of essay tests as compared with multiple-choice tests is that essay tests

   A. are more easily standardized
   B. allow for more creative responses
   C. can be completed in a shorter period of time
   D. are easier to score

9.____

10. When using a criterion-referenced test, student test scores should be compared with

    A. average statewide scores
    B. scores of other students
    C. a preset standard of mastery
    D. national norms

10.____

11. Which of the following should be the FIRST step in teaching material related to a new learning objective?

    A. Assign related readings
    B. Give a preview of new vocabulary
    C. Present the necessary information
    D. Explain the purpose of the lesson

11.____

12. A teacher plans to teach students how to locate resources in the school library.
How could the teacher approach this objective using didactic methodology?

    A. Encourage independent exploration to discover how library materials are organized
    B. Have students find materials through a process of trial and error
    C. Teach one skill at a time and provide frequent practice
    D. Give students a self-directed guide to using the library

12.____

13. A teacher has passed out reading material with a brief glossary of new words.
The BEST way to ensure that students understand the new words is to assign the students to

13.____

A. circle the new words where they occur in the text
B. read the material aloud to each other
C. write sentences using the new words
D. arrange the new words in alphabetical order

14. Good rapport between students and teachers is MOST likely to occur in classrooms in which

   A. rules are permissive
   B. students determine the pace of instruction
   C. decisions are made democratically
   D. teacher expectations are clear and reasonable

15. Which of the following is the MOST effective way to manage instruction for an elementary class involving students with a wide range of ability?

   A. Divide the class into small groups according to level
   B. Use the same materials for all students to challenge the weaker ones
   C. Assign extra work to those students who are furthest behind
   D. Work directly with the weakest students and ask others to work on their own

16. When applying discipline in an elementary school classroom, it is MOST important for the teacher to be

   A. compassionate   B. firm and strong
   C. consistent   D. broad-minded

17. In the school system, a MAJOR function of setting long-range educational goals is to

   A. provide overall direction for the curriculum
   B. make sure parents know what their children are learning
   C. find out what students need to learn
   D. eliminate repetition from one grade to another

18. According to the Family Educational Rights and Privacy Act, also known as the Buckley Amendment, parents have the right to

   A. select the public schools their children will attend
   B. inspect and review their children's educational records
   C. withhold information about their children from school officials
   D. attend classes with their children to monitor progress

KEY (CORRECT ANSWERS)

1. A
2. D
3. A
4. A
5. A

6. D
7. B
8. D
9. B
10. C

11. D
12. C
13. C
14. D
15. A

16. C
17. A
18. B

EXAMINATION SECTION
TEST 1

DIRECTIONS: Each question or incomplete statement is followed by several suggested answers or completions. Select the one that BEST answers the question or completes the statement. *PRINT THE LETTER OF THE CORRECT ANSWER IN THE SPACE AT THE RIGHT.*

Questions 1-5.

DIRECTIONS: In the following word groups, the *italicized* word at the left is followed by four lettered words or expressions. In each group, select the word or expression that MOST NEARLY defines the italicized word. *PRINT THE LETTER OF THE CORRECT ANSWER IN THE SPACE AT THE RIGHT.*

1. *Reluctance* 1.____
   - A. relief
   - B. unwillingness
   - C. forgetfulness
   - D. measure of light

2. *Relevant* 2.____
   - A. brotherly
   - B. disappearing
   - C. appropriate
   - D. ascending

3. *Mediator* 3.____
   - A. lawyer
   - B. intermediary
   - C. expert
   - D. official

4. *Jovial* 4.____
   - A. kingly
   - B. flattering
   - C. stern
   - D. jolly

5. *Ominous* 5.____
   - A. threatening
   - B. large
   - C. in transit
   - D. inclusive

Questions 6-10.

DIRECTIONS: In each of the following groups, one sentence contains an *italicized* word which makes the sentence INCORRECT. Select this sentence and print the letter in the space at the right.

6. 6.____
   - A. Congress *retrenched* its expenses by adding millions to the harbor improvement bill.
   - B. Thoreau found a way to *obviate* his dependence on money; he simplified his needs.
   - C. Under feudalism, an accepted *hierarchy* of social obligations made for political stability.
   - D. Long reflection, rather than sudden inspiration, is the *germinating* soil of great poetry.

7. A. The circus fat man is known as a man of *infinitesimal* bulk.
    B. The opening chapter of a mystery story contains *subtle* indications of the final outcome.
    C. A *tyro* sometimes surprises everyone by defeating the most experienced player.
    D. *Sporadic* outbursts of gunfire could be heard throughout the night.

8. A. His *infallibility* was the reason for his many errors and omissions.
    B. A soupy fog *encompassed* the huddled buildings of the big city.
    C. Efforts to *adjudicate* the disagreement were rejected by both parties.
    D. The development of his fortune was detailed in *chronological* order.

9. A. Atomic energy can be used effectively in the *desalinization* of ocean water.
    B. It was surprising that anyone should take *umbrage* at his joking remark.
    C. The conflicting points of view were at length *suffused* by the efforts of mediators.
    D. The guard's failure to appear was a *dereliction* of duty.

10. A. He *arrogated* to himself the privilege of selecting his successor.
    B. Many treaties provide for the *secession* of areas of land to one nation by another.
    C. His sweeping generalizations failed to *delineate* the problem.
    D. The legislature's failure to act on pollution was considered *deleterious* to the welfare of the people.

Questions 11-15.

DIRECTIONS: In each of the groups of four words, one is misspelled. Find the misspelled word in each group and print the letter of the CORRECT answer in the space at the right.

11. A. efficient
    B. received
    C. incandescent
    D. indefatigible

12. A. gossip
    B. seige
    C. resistance
    D. inoculate

13. A. orthadox
    B. probably
    C. coarse
    D. least

14. A. euphoria
    B. felon
    C. vengence
    D. morgue

15. A. oweing
    B. cancel
    C. satisfactorily
    D. communication

Questions 16-20.

DIRECTIONS: In each of the following groups of sentences, one of the four sentences is faulty in capitalization, punctuation, grammar, sentence structure, diction, etc. Select the INCORRECT sentence in each case and print the letter in the space at the right.

16. A. This list supersedes all previous notices.
     B. Unlike Susan, Frances has a calm disposition.
     C. The census report indicates that the village had fewer inhabitants in 1970 than in 1960.
     D. "Drive carefully," he warned. Speed is the cause of most accidents."

16.____

17. A. When I see John, I shall urge him to vote.
     B. The tyrant was hanged in effigy.
     C. The cinnamon bun tastes sweet.
     D. Turning the corner, the Leaning Tower came into view.

17.____

18. A. The reason for his illness is because he caught cold.
     B. Jack's brother said, "I don't think Jack will accept the nomination."
     C. Old people will feel the full effects of this ruling.
     D. Neither is a very competent secretary.

18.____

19. A. Get here at once - we need you!
     B. We gladly welcomed the Reverend John Baxter, D.D.
     C. We packed suits, dresses, coats, etc.
     D. He flouted the law, irregardless of its justice.

19.____

20. A. Football may be played in sunshine, snow, and when it rains.
     B. I'll be glad to enroll for that course, provided I get college credit for it.
     C. TALES OF A TRAVELER is among Washington Irving's best collections of short stories.
     D. Her manner, albeit disconcerting, is understandable.

20.____

Questions 21-75.

DIRECTIONS: In each of the following, select the one of the four lettered choices which will make the sentence *most nearly* CORRECT. Print the letter of the correct answer in the space at the right.

21. A ship's surgeon finds himself shipwrecked on the island of Lilliput in the novel

    A. THE PIRATE .... Sir Walter Scott
    B. GULLIVER'S TRAVELS .... Jonathan Swift
    C. RODERICK RANDOM .... Tobias Smollett
    D. BRIGHTON ROCK .... Graham Greene

21.____

22. The following musicals are all correctly matched with the work upon which they are based EXCEPT

    A. My Fair Lady .... CANDIDA
    B. Dear World .... THE MADWOMAN OF CHAILLOT
    C. Carousel .... LILIOM
    D. Man of La Mancha .... DON QUIXOTE

22.____

23. "For fools rush in where angels fear to _____" The word omitted in the above line by Alexander Pope is

   A. walk   B. stride   C. tread   D. go

24. All of the following were famous collaborators EXCEPT

   A. Rodgers and Hart
   B. Keats and Shelley
   C. Wordsworth and Coleridge
   D. Gilbert and Sullivan

25. "Hitch your wagon to a star" is a quotation from a work by

   A. Ralph W. Emerson
   B. David Thoreau
   C. James R. Lowell
   D. Horace Mann

26. An American writer of sea stories that are set in the South Pacific is

   A. Joseph Conrad
   B. Somerset Maugham
   C. William James
   D. Herman Melville

27. APOLOGY, CRITO, PHAEDO, and REPUBLIC are dialogues by

   A. Plato   B. Aristotle   C. Euripides   D. Menander

28. THE SHOES OF THE FISHERMAN by Morris West is

   A. an account of St. Peter and the Early Church
   B. the story of a Russian who became Bishop of Rome
   C. a biography of Izaak Walton
   D. a tale about a Japanese spy in World War II

29. The story in which a man is condemned to the Bastille because of his knowledge of the cruel treatment offered a peasant family is found in

   A. THE CRIME OF SYLVESTRE BONNARD . . . . Anatole France
   B. THE PLAGUE . . . . Albert Camus
   C. A TALE OF TWO CITIES . . . . Charles Dickens
   D. A LOST LADY . . . . Willa Gather

30. All of the following deal mainly with the theme of war EXCEPT

   A. JOURNEY'S END . . . . Robert C. Sherriff
   B. IDIOT'S DELIGHT . . . . Robert E. Sherwood
   C. HEARTBREAK HOUSE . . . . George B. Shaw
   D. THE SKIN OF OUR TEETH . . . . Thornton Wilder

31. Each of the following Black leaders is correctly matched with an activity for which he became famous EXCEPT

   A. Frederick Douglass . . . . writer
   B. Thurgood Marshall . . . . first Black Justice of the Supreme Court
   C. Nat Turner . . . . leader of a slave insurrection in Virginia in the 1830's
   D. Ralph Bunche . . . . President of Tuskegee Institute

32. Each of the following organizations was created by the United Nations EXCEPT the

    A. International Civil Aviation Organization
    B. International Labor Organization
    C. Food and Agricultural Organization
    D. World Health Organization

33. All of the following are famous straits EXCEPT

    A. Voringfoss
    B. Dardanelles
    C. Bosporus
    D. Gibraltar

34. Each of the following men was, at one time, a Chief Justice of the United States Supreme Court EXCEPT

    A. George C. Marshall
    B. William Howard Taft
    C. Salmon P. Chase
    D. John Jay

35. When census officials refer to the *missing Americans,* they are speaking of

    A. prisoners of war
    B. the many Black citizens uncounted in the 1960 census
    C. middle-class people who refuse to fill out the census forms
    D. the silent majority

36. Each of the following present or former prime ministers is matched correctly with his country EXCEPT

    A. Jomo Kenyatta .... Republic of South Africa
    B. Pierre Trudeau .... Canada
    C. Ian Smith........................ Rhodesia
    D. Edward Heath .... Great Britain

37. The section of Nigeria which recently failed to gain its independence in a civil war is known as

    A. Basutoland   B. Burundi   C. Mali   D. Biafra

38. The Mayor of New York has the power to

    A. fix the annual tax rate
    B. appoint the President of the City Council
    C. veto a budget adopted by the Board of Estimate and the City Council
    D. appoint the head of the Fire Department

39. Each of the following is a trend of our current economy EXCEPT

    A. a significant decrease in unemployment
    B. an increase in inflationary pressures
    C. high bank interest rates
    D. a decrease in the purchasing value of the dollar

40. The conduct of foreign affairs is entrusted by the American Constitution to the

    A. Secretary of State
    B. Senate's Committee on Foreign Affairs
    C. President
    D. House of Representatives.

41. The rate of metabolism in the human body is MOST closely associated with the activity of the

    A. adrenal glands   B. stomach
    C. pancreas   D. thyroid

42. A planet that has the fastest orbital speed around the sun is

    A. Pluto   B. Mercury   C. Jupiter   D. Neptune

43. The nutrient that is MOST useful for growth and repair of body cells is

    A. fats   B. sugar   C. starch   D. protein

44. Each of the following instruments is correctly associated with what it measures EXCEPT

    A. anemometer .... precipitation
    B. hygrometer .... humidity
    C. barograph .... air pressure
    D. seismograph .... earthquakes

45. All of the following statements concerning magnetism are correct EXCEPT:

    A. Any object that is attracted by a magnet becomes a magnet itself while in contact with the real magnet
    B. Like poles repel each other
    C. When a bar magnet is bent into a horseshoe, its strength increases
    D. When a bar magnet is cut in two, it loses one of its poles

46. The term *shuttlecook* refers to the object the players hit or strike at in the game of

    A. badminton   B. golf   C. hockey   D. tennis

47. Of the following ways of viewing a solar eclipse, the SAFEST is

    A. through sunglasses
    B. by looking through clear plastic
    C. indirectly
    D. through smoked glass

48. In tennis, the MINIMUM number of games necessary to complete a regulation set is

    A. two   B. four   C. six   D. eight

49. In the human circulatory system, the blood vessels that carry the blood AWAY from the heart are called

    A. veins   B. capillaries
    C. valves   D. arteries

50. All of the dances indicated below are correctly paired with their country of origin EXCEPT

    A. Tarantella...Spain
    B. Troika ....Russia
    C. La Raspa...Mexico
    D. Circassian Circle ....United States

51. A song in a minor key *usually* ends on

    A. do   B. sol   C. la   D. re

52. The YOUNG PERSON'S GUIDE TO THE ORCHESTRA was composed by

    A. Bernstein   B. Britten
    C. Kleinsinger   D. Prokofiev

53. The following are all sung in the MIKADO EXCEPT

    A. Three Little Maids From School
    B. I've Got a Little List
    C. I'm Called Little Buttercup
    D. Tit-Willow.

54. A dot following a note increases the note's value

    A. to twice its original value
    B. by an extra beat
    C. to three times its original value
    D. by half of its original value

55. All of the following composers are noted for their frequently produced operas EXCEPT

    A. A. Mozart   B. Haydn   C. Puccini   D. Wagner

56. Chichén Itzá, Monte Albán, and Mitla are Latin American sites renowned for

    A. displaying giant sculptural forms during the Olympic Games of recent years
    B. modern housing developments near Mexico City
    C. their ancient universities
    D. pre-Columbian (Hispanic) architecture

57. Of the following artists, the one known for his painting, BIRTH OF VENUS, depicting a beautiful maiden rising from a shell, is

    A. Fra Angelico   B. Cellini
    C. Botticelli   D. Raphael

58. Sargent, Lawrence, Stuart, and Van Dyke

    A. were Greenwich Village artists circa 1915
    B. are well known for their portraits
    C. were members of the Dutch School of artists
    D. are known for introducing distorted objects into their painting

59. On the Acropolis in Athens stand the remains of a glorious Greek temple known as the

    A. Parthenon   B. Onias   C. Pantheon   D. Karnak

60. Claude Monet, Camille Pissarro, and Auguste Renoir are generally classified as

   A. Dadaists
   B. Impressionists
   C. Abstractionists
   D. pottery makers

61. A store ran a sale, marking everything at 75% of the original price. A dress was sold at the sale for $48.00. Its original price was

   A. $36.00   B. $60.00   C. $64.00   D. $75.00

62. A roast requires 20 minutes of cooking time per pound. If the roast weighs 6 pounds and 12 ounces and is placed in the oven at 4:30 P.M., it should be ready at _____ P.M.

   A. 6:10   B. 6:45   C. 6:52   D. 7:22

63. The group which contains a number that is NOT prime is

   A. 21, 23, 29, 31
   B. 11, 13, 17, 19
   C. 2, 3, 5, 7
   D. 37, 41, 43, 47

64. A recipe for syrup calls for 1 1/2 cups of sugar to 3/4 cup of boiling water. Mrs. Jones has only 1 cup of sugar. She should use ____ cup of boiling water.

   A. 1/4   B. 1/3   C. 1/2   D. 5/6

65. If John is younger than 20 years of age and Mary is younger than 10 years of age, we may conclude that

   A. John is younger than Mary
   B. the combined ages of John and Mary cannot exceed 30
   C. John is twice as old as Mary
   D. John is older than Mary

66. A man drives 90 miles at an average of 30 miles per hour and returns to his starting point at an average of 45 miles per hour.
   His average rate for the round trip is _____ m.p.h.

   A. 40   B. 37 1/2   C. 36   D. 34

67. A baseball team has won 50 of the 75 games played thus far. There are 120 games in the entire season.
   How many more games must the team win to end with an average of 80% won?

   A. 40   B. 45   C. 46   D. 50

68. A bank customer borrowed $600 for one month. He paid $3.00 interest.
   What is the rate of interest for the month?

   A. .05%   B. .5%   C. 5%   D. 50%

69. The number missing in the series 3, 4, 7, 12, _____, 28 is

   A. 17   B. 19   C. 21   D. 22

70. A man left an estate of $24,000. According to his will, 10% went to a college, 15% to a hospital, with the remainder to be shared equally by four nieces. Each niece received

   A. $2,000   B. 3,600   C. $4,500   D. $6,000

71. A teacher wishes to show 30% of the circle on a circular graph. The central angle of that sector must be

 A. 50°   B. 54°   C. 90°   D. 108°

72. Of the packaged cereals listed below, all of equal quality, the MOST economical is

 A. 6 oz. for 15¢ B. 14 oz. for 34¢
 C. 1 lb. 3 oz. for 48¢ D. 2 lbs. for 75¢

73. The MOST common explanation given by the young addict for drug usage is

 A. an unstable family life
 B. that the problems of life fade away
 C. that it leads to acceptance by peers
 D. the thrill of committing an illegal act

74. The glue sniffer may *usually* be recognized by

 A. the way he picks sores constantly
 B. the way he licks his lips frequently
 C. his animated behavior with rapid, loud talking
 D. the odor of the substance inhaled on his breath or the clothes

75. The odor of marijuana smoke is frequently described as

 A. sour   B. sweetish   C. pungent   D. irritating

KEY (CORRECT ANSWERS)

1. B	16. D	31. D	46. A	61. C
2. C	17. D	32. B	47. C	62. B
3. B	18. A	33. A	48. C	63. A
4. D	19. D	34. A	49. D	64. C
5. A	20. A	35. B	50. A	65. B
6. A	21. B	36. A	51. C	66. C
7. A	22. A	37. D	52. D	67. C
8. A	23. C	38. D	53. C	68. B
9. C	24. B	39. A	54. D	69. B
10. B	25. A	40. C	55. B	70. C
11. D	26. D	41. D	56. D	71. D
12. B	27. A	42. B	57. C	72. D
13. A	28. B	43. D	58. B	73. C
14. C	29. C	44. A	59. A	74. D
15. A	30. D	45. D	60. B	75. B

READING COMPREHENSION
UNDERSTANDING AND INTERPRETING WRITTEN MATERIAL
EXAMINATION SECTION
TEST 1

DIRECTIONS: Each question or incomplete statement is followed by several suggested answers or completions. Select the one that BEST answers the question or completes the statement. *PRINT THE LETTER OF THE CORRECT ANSWER IN THE SPACE AT THE RIGHT.*

1. The National Assessment of Educational Progress recently released the results of the first statistically valid national sampling of young adult reading skills in the United States. According to the survey, ninety-five percent of United States young adults (aged 21-25) can read at a fourth-grade level or better. This means they can read well enough to apply for a job, understand a movie guide or join the Army. This is a higher literacy rate than the eighty to eighty-five percent usually estimated for all adults. The study also found that ninety-nine percent can write their names, eighty percent can read a map or write a check for a bill, seventy percent can understand an appliance warranty or write a letter about a billing error, twenty-five percent can calculate the amount of a tip correctly, and fewer than ten percent can correctly figure the cost of a catalog or understand a complex bus schedule.
Which statement about the study is BEST supported by the above passage?
   A. United States literacy rates among young adults are at an all-time high.
   B. Forty percent of young people in the United States cannot write a letter about a billing error.
   C. Twenty percent of United States teenagers cannot read a map,
   D. More than ninety percent of United States young adults cannot correctly calculate the cost of a catalog order.

1.____

2. It is now widely recognized that salaries, benefits, and working conditions have more of an impact on job satisfaction than on motivation. If they aren't satisfactory, work performance and morale will suffer. But even when they are high, employees will not necessarily be motivated to work well. For example, THE WALL STREET JOURNAL recently reported that as many as forty or fifty percent of newly hired Wall Street lawyers (whose salaries start at upwards of $50,000) quit within the first three years, citing long hours, pressures, and monotony as the prime offenders. It seems there's just not enough of an intellectual challenge in their jobs. An up and coming money-market executive concluded: *Whether it was $1 million or $100 million, the procedure was the same. Except for the tension, a baboon could do my job.* When money and benefits are adequate, the most important additional determinants of job satisfaction are: more responsibility, a sense of achievement, recognition, and a chance to advance. All of these factors have a more significant influence on employee motivation and performance. As a footnote, several studies have found that the absence of these non-monetary factors can lead to serious stress-related illnesses.

2.____

Which statement is BEST supported by the above passage?
- A. A worker's motivation to perform well is most affected by salaries, benefits, and working conditions.
- B. Low pay can lead to high levels of job stress.
- C. Work performance will suffer if workers feel they are not paid well.
- D. After satisfaction with pay and benefits, the next most important factor is more responsibility.

3. The establishment of joint labor-management production committees occurred in the United States during World War I and again during World War II. Their use was greatly encouraged by the National War Labor Board in World War I and the War Production Board in 1942. Because of the war, labor-management cooperation was especially desired to produce enough goods for the war effort, to reduce conflict, and to control inflation. The committees focused on how to achieve greater efficiency, and consulted on health and safety, training, absenteeism, and people issues in general. During the second world war, there were approximately five thousand labor-management committees in factories, affecting over six million workers. While research has found that only a few hundred committees made significant contributions to productivity, there were additional benefits in many cases. It became obvious to many that workers had ideas to contribute to the running of the organization, and that efficient enterprises could become even more so. Labor-management cooperation was also extended to industries that had never experienced it before. Directly after each war, however, few United States labor-management committees were in operation.

   Which statement is BEST supported by the above passage?
   - A. The majority of United States labor-management committees during the second world war accomplished little.
   - B. A major goal of United States labor-management committees during the first and second world wars was to increase productivity.
   - C. There were more United States labor-management committees during the second world war than during the first world war.
   - D. There are few United States labor-management committees in operation today.

4. Studies have found that stress levels among employees who have a great deal of customer contact or a great deal of contact with the public can be very high. There are many reasons for this. Sometimes stress results when the employee is caught in the middle—an organization wants things done one way, but the customer wants them done another way. The situation becomes even worse for the employee's stress levels when he or she knows was to more effectively provide the service, but isn't allowed to, by the organization. An example is the bank teller who is required to ask a customer for two forms of identification before he or she can cash a check, even though the teller knows the customer well. If organizational mishaps occur or if there are problems with job design, the employee may be powerless to satisfy the customer, and also powerless to protect himself or herself from the customer's wrath. An example of this is the waitress who is forced to serve poorly prepared food. Studies have also found,

however, that if the organization and the employee design the positions and the service encounter well, and encourage the use of effective stress management techniques, stress can be reduced to levels that are well below average.
Which statement is BEST supported by the above passage?
- A. It is likely that knowledgeable employees will experience greater levels of job-related stress.
- B. The highest levels of occupational stress are found among those employees who have a great deal of customer contact.
- C. Organizations can contribute to the stress levels of their employees by poorly designing customer contact situations.
- D. Stress levels are generally higher in banks and restaurants.

5. It is estimated that approximately half of the United States population suffers from varying degrees of adrenal malfunction. When under stress for long periods of time, the adrenals produce extra cortisol and norepinephrine. By producing more hormones than they were designed to comfortably manufacture and secrete, the adrenals can *burn out* over time and then decrease their secretion. When this happens, the body loses its capacity to cope with stress, and the individual becomes sicker more easily and for longer periods of time. A result of adrenal malfunction may be a diminished output of cortisol. Symptoms of diminished cortisol output include any of the following: craving substances that will temporarily raise serum glucose levels such as caffeine, sweets, soda, juice, or tobacco; becoming dizzy when standing up too quickly; irritability; headaches; and erratic energy levels. Since cortisol is an anti-inflammatory hormone, a decreased output over extended periods of time can make one prone to inflammatory disease such ass arthritis, bursitis, colitis, and allergies. (Many food and pollen allergies disappear when adrenal function is restored to normal.) The patient will have no reserve energy, and infections can spread quickly. Excessive cortisol production, on the other hand, can decrease immunity, leading to frequent and prolonged illnesses.
Which statement is BEST supported by the above passage?
- A. Those who suffer from adrenal malfunction are most likely to be prone to inflammatory diseases such as arthritis and allergies.
- B. The majority of Americans suffer from varying degrees of adrenal malfunction.
- C. It is better for the health of the adrenals to drink juice instead of soda.
- D. Too much cortisol can inhibit the body's ability to resist disease.

6. Psychologist B.F. Skinner pointed out long ago that gambling is reinforced either by design or accidentally, by what he called a variable ratio schedule. A slot machine, for example, is cleverly designed to provide a payoff after it has been played a variable number of times. Although the person who plays it and wins while playing receives a great deal of monetary reinforcement, over the long run the machine will take in much more money than it pays out. Research on both animals and humans has consistently found that such variable reward schedules maintain a very high rate of repeat behavior, and that this behavior is particularly resistant to extinction.

Which statement is BEST supported by the above passage?
A. Gambling, because it is reinforced by the variable ratio schedule, is more difficult to eliminate than most addictions.
B. If someone is rewarded or wins consistently, even if it is not that often, he or she is likely to continue that behavior.
C. Playing slot machines is the safest form of gambling because they are designed so that eventually the player will indeed win.
D. A cat is likely to come when called if its owner has trained it correctly.

7. Paper entrepreneurialism is an offshoot of scientific management that has become so extreme that it has lost all connection to the actual workplace. It generates profits by cleverly manipulating rules and numbers that only in theory represent real products and real assets. At its worst, paper entrepreneurialism involves very little more than imposing losses on others for the sake of short-term profits. The others may be taxpayers, shareholders who end up indirectly subsidizing other shar holders, consumers, or investors. Paper entrepreneurialism has replaced product entrepreneurialism, is seriously threatening the United States economy, and is hurting our necessary attempts to transform the nation's industrial and productive economic base. An example is the United States company that complained loudly in 1979 that it did not have the $200 million needed to develop a video-cassette recorder, though demand for them had been very high. The company, however, did not hesitate to spend $1.2 billion that same year to buy a mediocre finance company. The video recorder market was handed over to other countries, who did not hesitate to manufacture them.
Which statement is BEST supported by the above passage?
A. Paper entrepreneurialism involves very little more than imposing losses on others for the sake of short-term profits.
B. Shareholders are likely to benefit most from paper entrepreneurialism.
C. Paper entrepreneurialism is hurting the United States economy.
D. The United States could have made better video-cassette recorders than the Japanese but we ceded the market to them in 1979.

7._____

8. The *prisoner's dilemma* is an almost 40-year-old game-theory model psychologists, biologists, economists, and political scientists use to try to understand the dynamics of competition and cooperation. Participants in the basic version of the experiment are told that they and their *accomplice* have been caught red-handed. Together, their best strategy is to cooperate by remaining silent. If they do this, each will get off with a 30-day sentence. But either person can do better for himself or herself. If you double-cross your partner, you will go scot free while he or she serves ten years. The problem is, if you each betray the other, you will both go to prison for eight years, not thirty days. No matter what your partner chooses, you are logically better off choosing betrayal. Unfortunately, your partner realizes this too, and so the odds are good that you will both get eight years. That's the dilemma. (The length of the prison sentences is always the same for each variation.) Participants at a recent symposium on behavioral economics at Harvard University discussed the many variations on the game that have been used

8._____

over the years. In one standard version, subjects are paired with a supervisor who pays them a dollar for each point they score. Over the long run, both subjects will do best if they cooperate every time. Yet in each round, there is a great temptation to betray the other because no one knows what the other will do. The best overall strategy for this variation was found to be *tit for tat*, doing unto your opponent as he or she has just done unto you. It is a simple strategy, but very effective. The partner can easily recognize it and respond. It is retaliatory enough not to be easily exploited, but forgiving enough to allow a pattern of mutual cooperation to develop.
Which statement is BEST supported by the above passage?
- A. The best strategy for playing *prisoner's dilemma* is to cooperate and remain silent.
- B. If you double-cross your partner, and he or she does not double-cross you, your partner will receive a sentence of eight years.
- C. When playing *prisoner's dilemma*, it is best to double-cross your partner.
- D. If you double-cross your partner, and he or she double-crosses you, you will receive an eight-year sentence.

9. After many years of experience as the vice president and general manager of a large company, I feel that I know what I'm looking for in a good manager. First, the manager has to be comfortable with himself or herself, and not be arrogant or defensive. Secondly, he or she has to have a genuine interest in people. There are some managers who love ideas—and that's fine—but to be a manager, you must love people, and you must make a hobby of understanding them, believing in them and trusting them. Third, I look for a willingness and a facility to manage conflict. Gandhi defined conflict as a way of getting at the truth. Each person brings his or her own grain of truth and the conflict washes away the illusion and fantasy. Finally, a manager has to have a vision, and the ability and charisma to articulate it. A manager should be seen as a little bit crazy. Some eccentricity is an asset. People don't want to follow vanilla leaders. They want to follow chocolate-fudge-ripple leaders.
Which statement is BEST supported by the above passage?
- A. It is very important that a good manager spend time studying people.
- B. It is critical for good managers to love ideas.
- C. Managers should try to minimize or avoid conflict.
- D. Managers should be familiar with people's reactions to different flavors of ice cream.

9.____

10. Most societies maintain a certain set of values and assumptions that make their members feel either good or bad about themselves, and either better or worse than other people. In most developed countries, these values are based on the assumption that we are all free to be what we want to be, and that differences in income, work, and education are a result of our own efforts. This may make us believe that people with more income work that is more skilled, more education, and more power are somehow *better* people. We may view their achievements as proof that they have more intelligence, more motivation, and more initiative than those with lower status. The myth tells us that power, income, and education are freely and equally available to all, and that our

10.____

failure to achieve them is due to our own personal inadequacy. This simply is not the case.

The possessions we own may also seem to point to our real worth as individuals. The more we own, the more worthy of respect we may feel we are. Or, the acquisition of possessions may be a way of trying to fulfill ourselves, to make up for the loss of community and/or purpose. It is a futile pursuit because lost community and purpose can never be compensated for by better cars or fancier houses. And too often, when these things fail to satisfy, we believe it is only because we don't have enough money to buy better quality items, or more items. We feel bad that we haven't been successful enough to get all that we think we need. No matter how much we do have, goods never really satisfy for long. There is always something else to acquire, and true satisfaction eludes many, many of us.
Which statement is BEST supported by the above passage?
   A. The author would agree with the theory of *survival of the fittest*.
   B. The possessions an individual owns are not a proper measure of his or her real worth.
   C. Many countries make a sincere attempt to ensure equal access to quality education for their citizens.
   D. The effect a society's value system has on the lives of its members is greatly exaggerated.

11. *De nihilo nihil* is Latin for *nothing comes from nothing*. In the first century, the Roman poet Persius advised that if anything is to be produced of value, effort must be expended. He also said, *In nihilum nil posse revorti*—anything once produced cannot become nothing again. It is thought that Persius was parodying Lucretius, who expounded the 500-year-old physical theories of Epicurus. *De nihilo nihil* can also be used as a cynical comment, to negatively comment on something that is of poor quality produced by a person of little talent. The implication here is: *What can you expect from such a source?*
Which statement is BEST supported by the above passage?
   A. *In nihilum nil posse revorti* can be interpreted as meaning, *If anything is to be produced of value, then effort must be expended.*
   B. *De nihilo nihil* can be understood in two different ways,
   C. Lucretius was a great physicist.
   D. Persius felt that Epicurus put in little effort while developing his theories.

12. A Cornell University study has found that less than one percent of the billion pounds of pesticides used in this country annually strike their intended targets. The study found that the pesticides, which are somewhat haphazardly applied to 370 million acres, or about sixteen percent of the nation's total land area, end up polluting the environment and contaminating almost all 200,000 species of plants and animals, including humans. While the effect of indirect contamination on human cancer rates was not estimated, the study found that approximately 45,000 human pesticide poisonings occur annually, including about 3,000 cases admitted to hospitals and approximately 200 fatalities.

Which statement is BEST supported by the above passage?
- A. It is likely that indirect pesticide contamination affects human health.
- B. Pesticides are applied to over one-quarter of the total United States land area.
- C. If pesticides were applied more carefully, fewer pesticide-resistant strains of pests would develop.
- D. Human cancer rates in this country would drop considerably if pesticide use was cut in half.

13. The new conservative philosophy presents a unified, coherent approach to the world. It offers to explain much of our experience since the turbulent 1960s, and it shows what we've learned since about the dangers of indulgence and permissiveness. But it also warns that the world has become more ruthless, and that as individuals and as a nation, we must struggle for survival. It is necessary to impose responsibility and discipline in order to defeat those forces that threaten us. This lesson is dramatically clear, and can be applied to a wide range of issues.
    Which statement is BEST supported by the above passage?
    - A. The 1970s were a time of permissiveness and indulgence.
    - B. The new conservative philosophy may help in imposing discipline and a sense of responsibility in order to meet the difficult challenges facing this country.
    - C. The world faced greater challenges during the second world war than it faces at the present time.
    - D. More people identify themselves today as conservative in their political philosophy.

13.____

14. One of the most puzzling questions in management in recent years has been how usually honest, compassionate, intelligent managers can sometimes act in ways that are dishonest, uncaring, and unethical. How could top-level managers at the Manville Corporation, for example, suppress evidence for decades that proved beyond all doubt that asbestos inhalation was killing their own employees? What drove the managers of a Midwest bank to continue to act in a way that threatened to bankrupt the institution, ruin its reputation, and cost thousands of employees and investors their jobs and their savings? It's been estimated that about two out of three of America's five hundred largest corporations have been involved in some form of illegal behavior. There are, of course, some common rationalizations used to justify unethical conduct: believing that the activity is in the organization's or the individual's best interest, believing that the activity is not *really* immoral or illegal, believing that no one will ever know, or believing that the organization will sanction the behavior because it helps the organization. Ambition can distort one's sense of *duty*.
    Which statement is BEST supported by the above passage?
    - A. Top-level managers of corporations are currently involved in a plan to increase ethical behavior among their employees.
    - B. There are many good reasons why a manager may act unethically.
    - C. Some managers allow their ambitions to override their sense of ethics.
    - D. In order to successfully compete, some organizations may have to indulge in unethical or illegal behavior from time to time.

14.____

15. Some managers and supervisors believe that they are leaders because they occupy positions of responsibility and authority. But leadership is more than holding a position. It is often defined in management literature as *the ability to influence the opinions, attitudes and behaviors of others.* Obviously, there are some managers that would not qualify as leaders, and some leaders that are not *technically* managers. Research has found that many people overrate their own leadership abilities. In one recent study, seventy percent of those surveyed rated themselves in the top quartile in leadership abilities, and only two percent felt they were below average as leaders.

    Which statement is BEST supported by the above passage?
    A. In a recent study, the majority of people surveyed rated themselves in the top twenty-five percent in leadership abilities.
    B. Ninety-eight percent of the people surveyed in a recent study had average or above-average leadership skills.
    C. In order to be a leader, one should hold a management position.
    D. Leadership is best defined as the ability to be liked by those one must lead.

15.____

KEY (CORRECT ANSWERS)

1.	D	6.	B	11.	B
2.	C	7.	C	12.	A
3.	B	8.	D	13.	B
4.	C	9.	A	14.	C
5.	D	10.	B	15.	A

PREPARING WRITTEN MATERIALS
EXAMINATION SECTION
TEST 1

DIRECTIONS: Each question or incomplete statement is followed by several suggested answers or completions. Select the one that BEST answers the question or completes the statement. *PRINT THE LETTER OF THE CORRECT ANSWER IN THE SPACE AT THE RIGHT.*

Questions 1-21.

DIRECTIONS: In each of the following sentences, which were taken from students' transcripts, there may be an error. Indicate the appropriate correction in the space at the right. If the sentence is correct as is, indicate this choice. Unnecessary changes will be considered incorrect.

1. In that building there seemed to be representatives of Teachers College, the Veterans Bureau, and the Businessmen's Association.   1.____
    A. Teacher's College   B. Veterans' Bureau
    C. Businessmens Association   D. Correct as is

2. In his travels, he visited St. Paul, San Francisco, Springfield, Ohio, and Washington, D.C.   2.____
    A. Ohio and   B. Saint Paul
    C. Washington, D.C.   D. Correct as is

3. As a result of their purchasing a controlling interest in the syndicate, it was well-known that the Bureau of Labor Statistics' calculations would be unimportant.   3.____
    A. of them purchasing   B. well known
    C. Statistics   D. Correct as is

4. Walter Scott, Jr.'s, attempt to emulate his father's success was doomed to failure.   4.____
    A. Junior's,   B. Scott's, Jr.
    C. Scott, Jr.'s attempt   D. Correct as is

5. About B.C. 250 the Romans invaded Great Britain, and remains of their highly developed civilization can still be seen.   5.____
    A. 250 B.C.   B. Britain and
    C. highly-developed   D. Correct as is

6. The two boss's sons visited the children's department.   6.____
    A. bosses   B. bosses'   C. childrens'   D. Correct as is

7. Miss Amex not only approved the report, but also decided that it needed no revision.
   A. report; but   B. report but   C. report. But   D. Correct as is

8. Here's brain food in a jiffy—economical, too!
   A. economical too!   B. "brain food"
   C. jiffy-economical   D. Correct as is

9. She said, "He likes the "Gatsby Look" very much."
   A. said "He   B. "he
   C. 'Gatsby Look'   D. Correct as is

10. We anticipate that we will be able to visit them briefly in Los Angeles on Wednesday after a five day visit.
    A. Wednes-   B. 5 day   C. five-day   D. Correct as is

11. She passed all her tests, and, she now has a good position.
    A. tests, and she   B. past
    C. tests;   D. Correct as is

12. The billing clerk said, "I will send the bill today"; however, that was a week ago, and it hasn't arrived yet!
    A. today;"   B. today,"   C. ago and   D. Correct as is

13. "She types at more-than-average speed," Miss Smith said, "but I feel that it is a result of marvelous concentration and self control on her part."
    A. more than average   B. "But
    C. self-control   D. Correct as is

14. The state of Alaska, the largest state in the union, is also the northernmost state.
    A. Union   B. Northernmost State
    C. State of Alaska   D. Correct as is

15. The memoirs of Ex-President Nixon, according to figures, sold more copies than Six Crises, the book he wrote in the '60s.
    A. Six Crises   B. ex-President
    C. 60s   D. Correct as is

16. "There are three principal elements, determining the hazard of buildings: the contents hazard, the fire resistance of the structure, and the character of the interior finish," concluded the speaker.
    The one of the following statements that is MOST acceptable is that, in the above passage,
    A. the comma following the word *elements* is incorrect
    B. the colon following the word *buildings* is incorrect
    C. the comma following the word *finish* is incorrect
    D. there is no error in the punctuation of the sentence

17. He spoke on his favorite topic, "Why We Will Win." (How could I stop him?) 17.____
    A. Win". B. him?). C. him)? C. Correct as is

18. "All any insurance policy is, is a contract for services," said my insurance agent, Mr. Newton. 18.____
    A. Insurance Policy B. Insurance Agent
    C. policy is is a D. Correct as is

19. Inasmuch as the price list has now been up dated, we should sent it to the printer. 19.____
    A. In as much B. updated
    C. pricelist D. Correct as is

20. We feel that "Our know-how" is responsible for the improvement in technical developments. 20.____
    A. "our B. know how C. that, D. Correct as is

21. Did Cortez conquer the Incas? the Aztecs? the South American Indians? 21.____
    A. Incas, the Aztecs, the South American Indians?
    B. Incas; the Aztecs; the South American Indians?
    C. south American Indians?
    D. Correct as is

22. Which one of the following forms for the typed name of the dictator in the closing lines of a letter is generally MOST acceptable in the United States? 22.____
    A. (Dr.) James F. Farley B. Dr. James F. Farley
    C. Me. James J. Farley, Ph.D. D. James F. Farley

23. The plural of 23.____
    A. turkey is turkies B. cargo is cargoes
    C. bankruptcy is bankruptcys D. son-in-law is son-in-laws

24. The abbreviation viz. means MOST NEARLY 24.____
    A. namely B. for example
    C. the following D. see

25. In the sentence, *A man in a light-gray suit waited thirty-five minutes in the ante-room for the all-important document*, the word IMPROPERLY hyphenated is 25.____
    A. light-gray B. thirty-five C. ante-room D. all-important

KEY (CORRECT ANSWERS)

1. D
2. C
3. B
4. D
5. A

6. B
7. B
8. D
9. C
10. C

11. A
12. D
13. D
14. A
15. B

16. A
17. D
18. D
19. B
20. A

21. D
22. D
23. B
24. A
25. C

TEST 2

DIRECTIONS: Each question or incomplete statement is followed by several suggested answers or completions. Select the one that BEST answers the question or completes the statement. *PRINT THE LETTER OF THE CORRECT ANSWER IN THE SPACE AT THE RIGHT.*

Questions 1-10.

DIRECTIONS: In each of the following groups of four sentences, one sentence contains an error in sentence structure, grammar, usage, diction, or punctuation. Indicate the INCORRECT sentence.

1. A. The lecture finished, the audience began asking questions.
   B. Any man who could accomplish that task the world would regard as a hero.
   C. Our respect and admiration are mutual.
   D. George did like his mother told him, despite the importunities of his playmates.

2. A. I cannot but help admiring you for your dedication to your job.
   B. Because they had insisted upon showing us films of their travels, we have lost many friends whom we once cherished.
   C. I am constrained to admit that your remarks made me feel bad.
   D. My brother having been notified of his acceptance by the university of his choice, my father immediately made plans for a vacation.

3. A. In no other country is freedom of speech and assembly so jealously guarded.
   B. Being a beatnik, he felt that it would be a betrayal of his cause to wear shoes and socks at the same time.
   C. Riding over the Brooklyn Bridge gave us an opportunity to see the Manhattan skyline.
   D. In 1961, flaunting SEATO, the North Vietnamese crossed the line of demarcation.

4. A. I have enjoyed the study of the Spanish language not only because of its beauty and the opportunity it offers to understand the Hispanic culture but also to make use of it in the business associations I have in South America.
   B. The opinions he expressed were decidedly different from those he had held in his youth.
   C. Had he actually studied, he certainly would have passed.
   D. A supervisor should be patient, tactful, and firm.

5. A. At this point we were faced with only three alternatives: to push on, to remain where we were, or to return to the village.
   B. We had no choice but to forgive so venial a sin.
   C. In their new picture, the Warners are flouting tradition.
   D. Photographs taken revealed that 2.5 square miles had been burned.

6. A. He asked whether he might write to his friends.
    B. There are many problems which must be solved before we can be assured of world peace.
    C. Each person with whom I talked expressed his opinion freely.
    D. Holding on to my saddle with all my strength the horse galloped down the road at a terrifying pace.

7. A. After graduating high school, he obtained a position as a runner in Wall Street.
    B. Last night, in a radio address, the President urged us to subscribe to the Red Cross.
    C. In the evening, light spring rain cooled the streets.
    D. "Un-American" is a word which has been used even by those whose sympathies may well have been pro-Nazi.

8. A. It is hard to conceive of their not doing good work.
    B. Who won—you or I?
    C. He having read the speech caused much comment.
    D. Their finishing the work proves that it can be done.

9. A. Our course of study should not be different now than it was five years ago.
    B. I cannot deny myself the pleasure of publicly thanking the mayor for his actions.
    C. The article on "Morale" has appeared in the Times Literary Supplement.
    D. He died of tuberculosis contracted during service with the Allied Forces.

10. A. If it wasn't for a lucky accident, he would still be an office-clerk.
    B. It is evident that teachers need help.
    C. Rolls of postage stamps may be bought at stationery stores.
    D. Addressing machines are used by firms that publish magazines.

11. The one of the following sentences which contains NO error in usage is:
    A. After the robbers left, the proprietor stood tied in his chair for about two hours before help arrived.
    B. In the cellar I found the watchmans' hat and coat.
    C. The persons living in adjacent apartments stated that they had heard no unusual noises.
    D. Neither a knife or any firearms were found in the room.

12. The one of the following sentences which contains NO error in usage is:
    A. The policeman lay a firm hand on the suspect's shoulder.
    B. It is true that neither strength nor agility are the most important requirement for a good patrolman.
    C. Good citizens constantly strive to do more than merely comply the restraints imposed by society.
    D. Twenty years is considered a severe sentence for a felony.

13. Select the sentence containing an adverbial objective.   13._____
    A. Concepts can only acquire content when they are connected, however indirectly, with sensible experience.
    B. The cloth was several shades too light to match the skirt which she had discarded.
    C. The Gargantuan Hall of Commons became a tri-daily horror to Kurt, because two youths discerned that he had a beard and courageously told the world about it.
    D. Brooding morbidly over the event, Elsie found herself incapable of engaging in normal activity.

14. Select the sentence containing a verb in the subjunctive mood.   14._____
    A. Had he known of the new experiments with penicillin dust for the cure of colds, he might have been tempted to try them in his own office.
    B. I should be very much honored by your visit.
    C. Though he has one of the highest intelligence quotients in his group, he seems far below the average in actual achievement.
    D. Long had I known that he would be the man finally selected for such signal honors.

15. Select the sentence containing one (or more) passive perfect participle(s).   15._____
    A. Having been apprised of the consequences of his refusal to answer, the witness finally revealed the source of his information.
    B. To have been placed in such an uncomfortable position was perhaps unfair to a journalist of his reputation.
    C. When deprived of special immunity he had, of course, no alternative but to speak.
    D. Having been obdurate until now, he was reluctant to surrender under this final pressure exerted upon him.

16. Select the sentence containing a predicate nominative.   16._____
    A. His dying wish, which he expressed almost with his last breath, was to see that justice was done toward his estranged wife.
    B. So long as we continue to elect our officials in truly democratic fashion, we shall have the power to preserve our liberties.
    C. We could do nothing, at this juncture, but walk the five miles back to camp.
    D. There was the spaniel, wet and cold and miserable, waiting silently at the door.

17. Select the sentence containing exactly TWO adverbs.   17._____
    A. The gentlemen advanced with exasperating deliberateness, while his lonely partner waited.
    B. If you are well, will you come early?
    C. I think you have guessed right, though you were rather slow, I must say.
    D. The last hundred years have seen more change than a thousand years of the Roman Empire, than a hundred thousand years of the stone age.

Questions 18-24.

DIRECTIONS: Select the choice describing the error in the sentence.

18. If us seniors do not support school functions, who will?
    A. Unnecessary shift in tense
    B. Incomplete sentence
    C. Improper case of pronoun
    D. Lack of parallelism

19. The principal has issued regulations which, in my opinion, I think are too harsh.
    A. Incorrect punctuation
    B. Faulty sentence structure
    C. Misspelling
    D. Redundant expression

20. The freshmens' and sophomores' performances equaled those of the juniors and seniors.
    A. Ambiguous reference
    B. Incorrect placement of punctuation
    C. Misspelling of past tense
    D. Incomplete comparison

21. Each of them, Anne and her, is an outstanding pianist I can't tell you which one is best.
    A. Lack of agreement
    B. Improper degree of comparison
    C. Incorrect case of pronoun
    D. Run-on sentence

22. She wears clothes that are more expensive than my other friends.
    A. Misuse of *than*
    B. Incorrect relative pronoun
    C. Shift in tense
    D. Faulty comparison

23. At the very end of the story it implies that the children's father died tragically.
    A. Misuse of *implies*
    B. Indefinite use of pronoun
    C. Incorrect spelling
    D. Incorrect possessive

24. At the end of the game both of us, John and me, couldn't scarcely walk because we were so tired.
    A. Incorrect punctuation
    B. Run-on sentence
    C. Incorrect case of pronoun
    D. Double negative

Questions 25-30.

DIRECTIONS: Questions 25 through 30 consist of a sentence lacking certain needed punctuation. Pick as your answer the description of punctuation which will CORRECTLY complete the sentence.

25. If you take the time to keep up your daily correspondence you will no doubt be most efficient.
    A. Comma only after *doubt*
    B. Comma only after *correspondence*
    C. Commas after *correspondence*, *will*, and *be*
    D. Commas after *if*, *correspondence*, and *will*

26. Because he did not send the application soon enough he did not receive the up to date copy of the book. 26.____
    A. Commas after *application* and *enough*, and quotation marks before *up* and after *date*
    B. Commas after *application* and *enough*, and hyphens between *to* and *date*
    C. Comma after *enough*, and hyphens between *up* and *to* and between *to* and *date*
    D. Comma after *application*, and quotation marks before *up* and after *date*

27. The coordinator requested from the department the following items a letter each week summarizing progress personal forms and completed applications for tests. 27.____
    A. Commas after *items* and *completed*
    B. Semi-colon after *items* and *progress*, comma after *forms*
    C. Colon after *items*, commas after *progress* and *forms*
    D. Colon after *items*, commas after *forms* and *applications*

28. The supervisor asked Who will attend the conference next month. 28.____
    A. Comma after *asked*, period after *month*
    B. Period after *asked*, question mark after *month*
    C. Comma after *asked*, quotation marks before *Who*, quotation marks after *month*, and question mark after the quotation marks
    D. Comma after *asked*, quotation marks before *Who*, question mark after *month*, and quotation marks after the question mark

29. When the statistics are collected, we will forward the results to you as soon as possible. 29.____
    A. Comma after *you*
    B. Commas after *forward* and *you*
    C. Commas after *collected*, *results* and *you*
    D. Comma after *collected*

30. The ecology of our environment is concerned with mans pollution of the atmosphere. 30.____
    A. Comma after *ecology*
    B. Apostrophe after *n* and before *s* in *mans*
    C. Commas after *ecology* and *environment*
    D. Apostrophe after *s* in *mans*

KEY (CORRECT ANSWERS)

1.	D	11.	C	21.	B
2.	A	12.	D	22.	D
3.	D	13.	B	23.	B
4.	A	14.	A	24.	D
5.	B	15.	A	25.	B
6.	D	16.	A	26.	C
7.	A	17.	C	27.	C
8.	C	18.	C	28.	D
9.	A	19.	D	29.	D
10.	A	20.	B	30.	B

TEST 3

DIRECTIONS: Each question or incomplete statement is followed by several suggested answers or completions. Select the one that BEST answers the question or completes the statement. *PRINT THE LETTER OF THE CORRECT ANSWER IN THE SPACE AT THE RIGHT.*

Questions 1-6.

DIRECTIONS: From the four choices offered in Questions 1 through 6, select the one which is INCORRECT.

1.
   A. Before we try to extricate ourselves from this struggle in which we are now engaged in, we must be sure that we are not severing ties of honor and duty.
   B. Besides being an outstanding student, he is also a leader in school government and a trophy-winner in school sports.
   C. If the framers of the Constitution were to return to life for a day, their opinion of our amendments would be interesting.
   D. Since there are three m's in the word, it is frequently misspelled.

   1.____

2.
   A. It was a college with an excellance beyond question.
   B. The coach will accompany the winners, whomever they may be.
   C. The dean, together with some other faculty members, is planning a conference.
   D. The jury are arguing among themselves.

   2.____

3.
   A. This box is less nearly square than that one.
   B. Wagner is many persons' choice as the world's greatest composer.
   C. The habits of Copperheads are different from Diamond Backs.
   D. The teacher maintains that the child was insolent.

   3.____

4.
   A. There was a time when the Far North was unknown territory. Now American soldiers manning radar stations there wave to Boeing jet planes zooming by overhead.
   B. Exodus, the psalms, and Deuteronomy are all books of the Old Testament.
   C. Linda identified her china dishes by marking their bottoms with india ink.
   D. Harry S. Truman, former president of the United States, served as a captain in the American army during World War I.

   4.____

5.
   A. The sequel of their marriage was a divorce.
   B. We bought our car secondhand.
   C. His whereabouts is unknown.
   D. Jones offered to use his own car, providing the company would pay for gasoline, oil, and repairs,

   5.____

6. A. I read Golding's "Lord of the Flies".
    B. The orator at the civil rights rally thrilled the audience when he said, "I quote Robert Burns's line, 'A man's a man for a' that."
    C. The phrase "producer to consumer" is commonly used by market analysts.
    D. The lawyer shouted, "Is not this evidence illegal?"

Questions 7-9.

DIRECTIONS: In answering Questions 7 through 9, mark the letter A if faulty because of incorrect grammar, mark the letter B if faulty because of incorrect punctuation, mark the letter C if correct.

7. Mr. Brown our accountant, will audit the accounts next week.

8. Give the assignment to whomever is able to do it most efficiently.

9. The supervisor expected either your or I to file these reports.

Questions 10-14.

DIRECTIONS: In each of the following groups of four sentences, one sentence contains an error in sentence structure, grammar, usage, diction, or punctuation. Indicate the INCORRECT sentence.

10. A. The agent asked, "Did you say, 'Never again?'"
    B. Kindly let me know whether you can visit us on the 17th.
    C. "I cannot accept that!" he exploded. "Please show me something else.
    D. Ed, will you please lend me your grass shears for an hour or so.

11. A. Recalcitrant though he may have been, Alexander was willfully destructive.
    B. Everybody should look out for himself.
    C. John is one of those students who usually spends most of his time in the principal's office.
    D. She seems to feel that what is theirs is hers.

12. A. Be he ever so much in the wrong, I'll support the man while deploring his actions.
    B. The schools' lack of interest in consumer education is shortsighted.
    C. I think that Fitzgerald's finest stanza is one which includes the reference to youth's "sweet-scented manuscript.
    D. I never would agree to Anderson having full control of the company's policies.

13. A. We had to walk about five miles before finding a gas station.
    B. The willful sending of a false alarm has, and may, result in homicide.
    C. Please bring that book to me at once.
    D. Neither my sister nor I am interested in bowling.

14. A. He is one of the very few football players who doesn't wear a helmet with a face guard.
    B. But three volunteers appeared at the recruiting office.
    C. Such consideration as you can give us will be appreciated.
    D. When I left them, the group were disagreeing about the proposed legislation.

14.____

Question 15.

DIRECTIONS: Question 15 contains two sentences concerning criminal law. The sentences could contain errors in English grammar or usage. A sentence does not contain an error simply because it could be written in a different manner. In answering this question, choose answer
A. if only sentence I is correct
B. if only sentence II is correct
C. if both sentences are correct
D. if neither sentence is correct

15. I. The use of fire or explosives to destroy tangible property is proscribed by the criminal mischief provisions of the Revised Penal Law.
    II. The defendant's taking of a taxicab for the immediate purpose of affecting his escape did not constitute grand larceny.

15.____

KEY (CORRECT ANSWERS)

1.	A	6.	A	11.	C
2.	B	7.	B	12.	D
3.	C	8.	A	13.	B
4.	B	9.	A	14.	A
5.	D	10	A	15.	A

EXAMINATION SECTION
TEST 1

DIRECTIONS: Each question or incomplete statement is followed by several suggested answers or completions. Select the one that BEST answers the question or completes the statement. *PRINT THE LETTER OF THE CORRECT ANSWER IN THE SPACE AT THE RIGHT.*

Questions 1-25.

DIRECTIONS: Select the word with the MOST appropriate meaning for the italicized word in each of Questions 1 through 25.

1. The directions were *explicit*. 1.____
   A. petulant   B. satiric   C. awkward
   D. unequivocal   E. foreign

2. The teacher explained *mutability*. 2.____
   A. change   B. harmony   C. annihilation
   D. ethics   E. candor

3. He was a *secular* man. 3.____
   A. holy   B. evil   C. worldly
   D. superior   E. small

4. They submitted a list of their *progeny*. 4.____
   A. experiments   B. books   C. holdings
   D. theories   E. offspring

5. She admired his *sententious* replies. 5.____
   A. simple   B. pithy   C. coherent
   D. lucid   E. inane

6. He believed in the ancient *dogma*. 6.____
   A. priest   B. prophet   C. seer
   D. doctrine   E. ruler

7. They studied a Grecian *archetype*. 7.____
   A. model   B. urn   C. epic   D. ode   E. play

8. The *insurrection* was described on the front page. 8.____
   A. surgery   B. pageant   C. ceremony
   D. game   E. revolt

9. He was known for his *procrastination*. 9.____
   A. justification   B. learning   C. delay
   D. ambition   E. background

10. The doctor analyzed the *toxic* ingredients.
    A. poisonous
    B. anemic
    C. trivial
    D. obscure
    E. distinct

11. It was a *portentous* occurrence.
    A. pleasant
    B. decisive
    C. ominous
    D. monetary
    E. hearty

12. His *espousal* of the plan was applauded.
    A. explanation
    B. rejection
    C. ridicule
    D. adoption
    E. revision

13. Her condition was *lachrymose*.
    A. improved
    B. tearful
    C. hopeful
    D. precocious
    E. tenuous

14. It was a *precarious* situation.
    A. uncomplicated
    B. peaceful
    C. precise
    D. uncertain
    E. precipitous

15. He was lost in a *reverie*.
    A. chancery
    B. dream
    C. forest
    D. cavern
    E. tarn

16. The hero was a young *gallant*.
    A. suitor
    B. fool
    C. gull
    D. lawyer
    E. executive

17. Their practices were *nefarious*.
    A. unprofitable
    B. ignorant
    C. multifarious
    D. wicked
    E. wishful

18. He insisted upon the *proviso*.
    A. stipulation
    B. pronunciation
    C. examination
    D. supply
    E. equipment

19. The spirit came from the *nether* regions.
    A. frozen
    B. lower
    C. lost
    D. bright
    E. mysterious

20. His actions were *malevolent*.
    A. unassuming
    B. silent
    C. evil
    D. peaceful
    E. constructive

21. He had a *florid* complexion.
    A. sanguine
    B. pallid
    C. fair
    D. sickly
    E. normal

22. The lawyer explained the legal *parlance*.   22.____
    A. action   B. maneuver   C. situation
    D. language   E. procedure

23. They were present at the *interment*.   23.____
    A. concert   B. trial   C. embarkation
    D. burial   E. performance

24. He made a *moot* point.   24.____
    A. definite   B. sensible   C. debatable
    D. strong   E. correct

25. They carefully examined the *cryptic* message.   25.____
    A. occult   B. legible   C. valid
    D. familiar   E. warning

Questions 26-40.

DIRECTIONS: Indicate the number of syllables in each of the following words.

26. vicissitude   26.____

27. blown   27.____

28. maintenance   28.____

29. symbolization   29.____

30. athletics   30.____

31. actually   31.____

32. friend   32.____

33. perseverance   33.____

34. physiology   34.____

35. pronunciation   35.____

36. vacuum   36.____

37. sophomore   37.____

38. opportunity   38.____

39. hungry   39.____

40. temperament   40.____

Questions 41-60.

DIRECTIONS: Indicate the one misspelled work in each of the following Questions 41 through 60 by indicating the letter of the misspelled word in the space at the right.

41. A. holiday   B. noticeable   C. fourty   41._____
    D. miniature E. yeast

42. A. grievance B. murmur   C. occurance   42._____
    D. business E. captain

43. A. succeed   B. vegatable   C. pleasant   43._____
    D. picnicking E. shepherd

44. A. psychology B. plebian   C. exercise   44._____
    D. fiery   E. concise

45. A. ninety   B. optimistic   C. professor   45._____
    D. repitition E. siege

46. A. tarriff   B. absence   C. grammar   46._____
    D. license   E. balloon

47. A. dissipation B. ecstasy   C. prarie   47._____
    D. marriage E. consistent

48. A. supersede B. twelfth   C. vacillate   48._____
    D. playright E. expense

49. A. fundamental B. government C. accomodate   49._____
    D. cafeteria E. surely

50. A. cemetary B. indispensable C. dormitory   50._____
    D. environment E. divine

51. A. irritible B. permissible C. irresistible 51._____
    D. rhythmical E. source

52. A. interprete B. opinion   C. guard   52._____
    D. familiar E. possible

53. A. conscience B. existence   C. loneliness   53._____
    D. leisure   E. exhileration

54. A. villian   B. weird   C. seize   54._____
    D. tragedy   E. crystal

55. A. develop   B. bachelor   C. dilemma   55._____
    D. operate   E. synonym

5 (#1)

56. A. university   B. connoiseur   C. aisle   56._____
    D. transferred   E. division

57. A. zoology   B. conscious   C. aptitude   57._____
    D. restaurant   E. sacriligious

58. A. tendency   B. vital   C. analyze   58._____
    D. consistant   E. proceed

59. A. proceedure   B. surround   C. disastrous   59._____
    D. beginning   E. arrival

60. A. encrease   B. pursuing   C. necessary   50._____
    D. tyranny   E. strength

Questions 61-80.

DIRECTIONS: Indicate the part of speech for each italicized word in the following sentences by selecting the letter of the part of speech from the key above each set of questions.

   A. Noun
   B. Pronoun
   C. Verb
   D. Adjective
   E. Adverb

61. You are entirely *wrong*.   61._____

62. On *Sunday*, we will attend church.   62._____

63. *That* is the main problem.   63._____

64. He was invited to the party, *Saturday*.   64._____

65. I shall introduce a *technical* term.   65._____

66. It was a *novel* turn of events.   66._____

67. He wanted *that* gift for himself.   67._____

68. A few definitions will help *us* to understand.   68._____

69. He let them reach their own *conclusions*.   69._____

70. I must ask *you* to remain silent.   70._____

A. Preposition
B. Conjunction
C. Pronoun
D. Adverb
E. Adjective

71. *This* is a stupid answer.   71._____

72. He solved the mystery *without* the police.   72._____

73. She felt *secure* in his protection,   73._____

74. He believed in the *scientific* method.   74._____

75. Do not destroy their *traditional* beliefs.   75._____

76. They chartered the bus, *but* they did not go.   76._____

77. The young men are *quiet* with fear.   77._____

78. She talked *cheerfully* to the visitors.   78._____

79. The candidate was *certain* of victory.   79._____

80. I hope you will take *that* with you.   80._____

Questions 81-100.

DIRECTIONS: Indicate the use of each italicized word in the following sentences by choosing the letter of the CORRECT usage from the key above each set of questions.

A. Subject of Verb
B. Predicate Nominative or Subjective Complement
C. Predicate Adjective
D. Direct Object of Verb
E. Indirect Object of Verb

81. They made *him* president of the club.   81._____

82. There was nothing *odd* about the situation.   82._____

83. Give them *time* enough for thought.   83._____

84. He supervised the *work* himself.   84._____

85. Will you do *me* a favor?   85._____

86. The salad dressing tasted *good*.   86._____

7 (#1)

87. In the crash, the *body* was thrown forward.   87.____

88. On a bench in the park was a single *man*.   88.____

89. There were two *men* who carried the trunk.   89.____

90. I am older than *you*.   90.____

        A. Object of Preposition
        B. Subject of Infinitive
        C. Direct Object of Verb
        D. Indirect Object of Verb
        E. Predicate Nominative or Subjective Complement

91. Let *them* suffer the consequences.   91.____

92. Offer *them* the key to the apartment.   92.____

93. He heard the *bell* ring.   93.____

94. Let *us* try another solution.   94.____

95. No one except *John* had volunteered.   95.____

96. Show *us* one example of your style.   96.____

97. Will you send *her* the flowers?   97.____

98. I want *you* to take her home.   98.____

99. He told his *father* that he would obey.   99.____

100. Do not write on the second *page*.   100.____

Questions 101-115.

DIRECTIONS: Indicate the kind of verbal italicized in the following sentences by choosing the appropriate letter from the key below.

        A. Gerund
        B. Participle
        C. Infinitive

101. The manuscript, *corrected* and typed, was on the desk.   101.____

102. He heard the bullet *ricochet*.   102.____

103. *Finding* the answer is a difficult task.   103.____

104. The animal, *hidden* from view, was trembling.   104.____

105. *Pretending* to be asleep, he listened attentively.   105.____

106. The professor, a *qualified* lecturer, entered the room.   106.____

107. They enjoyed *camping* at the lake.   107.____

108. Let them *come* to me.   108.____

109. He was annoyed by the *buzzing* sound.   109.____

110. It was a *stimulating* performance.   110.____

111. He had an accident while *returning* to the city.   111.____

112. *Encouraged* to study, the class opened the books.   112.____

113. He heard the gun *explode*.   113.____

114. They called him the *forgotten* man.   114.____

115. *Realizing* his mistake, he apologized.   115.____

Questions 116-130.

DIRECTIONS: Indicate the CORRECT punctuation for the following sentences by choosing the letter of the correct punctuation from the key below where brackets appear.

    A. Comma
    B. Semicolon
    C. Colon
    D. Dash
    E. No punctuation

116. He explained [ ] that he could not attend.   116.____

117. The executive [ ] prepared for the interview and entered the room.   117.____

118. She admitted [ ] that the suggestion was wrong.   118.____

119. He did not object [ ] to dealing with him.   119.____

120. The chairman disagreed [ ] the members did not.   120.____

121. You must report to duty on November 10 [ ] 2022.   121.____

122. The father [ ] and two sons went fishing.   122.____

123. Act on the following problems [ ] administration, supervision, and policy. 123.____

124. This is excellent [ ] it has insight. 124.____

125. "I will take the car [ ]" he said. 125.____

126. I will do it [ ] however, you must help me. 126.____

127. When the show ended [ ] he returned home. 127.____

128. Stop [ ] making all of that noise. 128.____

129. Be firm [ ] exercise your authority. 129.____

130. The first example is poor [ ] the second is good. 130.____

Questions 131-150.

DIRECTIONS: Place a *C* in the space at the right if the sentence is correctly punctuated and a *W* in the space at the right if the sentence is incorrectly punctuated.

131. Its later than you think. 131.____

132. While I was eating the toast burned. 132.____

133. The fire started at ten o'clock in the morning. 133.____

134. She asked, "Did you say, 'I will go?" 134.____

135. Richards handling of the question warranted praise. 135.____

136. July 4 is a holiday. 136.____

137. Oh perhaps you are right. 137.____

138. Will you answer the door, John? 138.____

139. While he was bathing the dog came in. 139.____

140. He was a calm gentle person. 140.____

141. He wore a new bow tie. 141.____

142. The shout "Block that kick" echoed upon the field. 142.____

143. Ladies and gentlemen take your seats. 143.____

144. However you must do your work. 144.____

10 (#1)

145. My brothers are: John, Bill, and Charles. 145.____

146. While I was painting the neighbor opened the door. 146.____

147. One should fight for honor: not fame. 147.____

148. "Will you sing" he asked? 148.____

149. He played tennis, and then bowled. 149.____

150. On Monday April 5, we leave for Europe. 150.____

KEY (CORRECT ANSWERS)

1.	D	31.	4	61.	D	91.	C	121.	A
2.	A	32.	1	62.	A	92.	D	122.	E
3.	C	33.	4	63.	B	93.	C	123.	C
4.	E	34.	5	64.	A	94.	C	124.	D
5.	B	35.	5	65.	D	95.	A	125.	A
6.	D	36.	2	66.	D	96.	C	126.	B
7.	A	37.	3	67.	D	97.	C	127.	A
8.	E	38.	5	68.	B	98.	C	128.	E
9.	C	39.	2	69.	A	99.	C	129.	B
10.	A	40.	3	70.	B	100.	A	130.	B
11.	C	41.	C	71.	C	101.	B	131.	W
12.	D	42.	C	72.	A	102.	B	132.	W
13.	B	43.	B	73.	D	103.	A	133.	C
14.	D	44.	B	74.	E	104.	B	134.	W
15.	B	45.	D	75.	E	105.	A	135.	W
16.	A	46.	A	76.	B	106.	B	136.	C
17.	D	47.	C	77.	E	107.	A	137.	W
18.	A	48.	D	78.	D	108.	C	138.	C
19.	B	49.	C	79.	E	109.	B	139.	W
20.	C	50.	A	80.	C	110.	B	140.	W
21.	A	51.	A	81.	D	111.	A	141.	C
22.	D	52.	A	82.	C	112.	B	142.	W
23.	D	53.	E	83.	D	113.	C	143.	W
24.	C	54.	A	84.	D	114.	B	144.	W
25.	A	55.	C	85.	E	115.	A	145.	W
26.	3	56.	B	86.	C	116.	E	143.	W
27.	1	57.	E	87.	A	117.	E	147.	W
28.	3	58.	D	88.	B	118.	E	148.	W
29.	5	59.	A	89.	A	119.	E	149.	W
30.	3	60.	A	90.	C	120.	B	150.	W

EXAMINATION SECTION
TEST 1

DIRECTIONS: Each question or incomplete statement is followed by several suggested answers or completions. Select the one that BEST answers the question or completes the statement. *PRINT THE LETTER OF THE CORRECT ANSWER IN THE SPACE AT THE RIGHT.*

Questions 1-22.

DIRECTIONS: Read through each group of words. Indicate in the space at the right the letter of the misspelled word.

1. A. miniature   B. recession   1.____
    C. accommodate   D. supress

2. A. mortgage   B. illogical   2.____
    C. fasinate   D. pronounce

3. A. calendar   B. heros   3.____
    C. ecstasy   D. librarian

4. A. initiative   B. extraordinary   4.____
    C. villian   D. exaggerate

5. A. absence   B. sense   5.____
    C. dosn't   D. height

6. A. curiosity   B. ninety   6.____
    C. truely   D. grammar

7. A. amateur   B. definate   7.____
    C. meant   D. changeable

8. A. excellent   B. studioes   8.____
    C. achievement   D. weird

9. A. goverment   B. description   9.____
    C. sergeant   D. desirable

10. A. proceed   B. anxious   10.____
    C. neice   D. precede

11. A. environment   B. omitted   11.____
    C. apparant   D. misconstrue

12. A. comparative   B. hindrance   12.____
    C. benefited   D. unamimous

13. A. embarrass B. recommend 13.____
    C. desciple   D. argument

14. A. sophomore   B. suprintendent 14.____
    C. concievable D. disastrous

15. A. agressive   B. questionnaire 15.____
    C. occurred   D. rhythm

16. A. peaceable   B. conscientious 16.____
    C. redicule   D. deterrent

17. A. mischievious B. writing   17.____
    C. competition D. athletics

18. A. auxiliary   B. synonymous   18.____
    C. maneuver   D. repitition

19. A. existence   B. optomistic   19.____
    C. acquitted   D. tragedy

20. A. hypocrisy   B. parrallel   20.____
    C. exhilaration D. prevalent

21. A. convalesence B. infallible   21.____
    C. destitute   D. grotesque

22. A. magnanimity B. asassination   22.____
    C. incorrigible D. pestilence

Questions 23-40.

DIRECTIONS: In Questions 23 through 40, one sentence fragment contains an error in punctuation or capitalization. Indicate the letter of the INCORRECT sentence fragment and place it in the space at the right.

23. A. Despite a year's work   23.____
    B. in a well-equipped laboratory
    C. my Uncle failed to complete his research
    D. now he will never graduate.

24. A. Gene, if you are going to sleep   24.____
    B. all afternoon I will enter
    C. that ladies' golf tournament
    D. sponsored by the Chamber of Commerce.

25. A. Seeing the cat slink toward the barn,
    B. the farmer's wife jumped off the
    C. ladder picked up a broom, and began
    D. shouting at the top of her voice.

    25.____

26. A. Extending over southeast Idaho and
    B. northwest Wyoming, the Tetons
    C. are noted for their height; however the
    D. highest peak is actually under 14,000 feet.

    26.____

27. A. "Sarah, can you recall the name
    B. of the English queen
    C. who supposedly said, 'We are not
    D. amused?"

    27.____

28. A. My aunt's graduation present to me
    B. cost, I imagine more than she could
    C. actually afford. It's a
    D. Swiss watch with numerous features.

    28.____

29. A. On the left are examples of buildings
    B. from the Classical Period; two temples
    C. one of which was dedicated to Zeus; the
    D. Agora, a marketplace; and a large arch.

    29.____

30. A. Tired of sonic booms, the people who
    B. live near Springfield's Municipal Airport
    C. formed an anti noise organization
    D. with the amusing name of Sound Off.

    30.____

31. A. "Joe, Mrs. Sweeney said, "your family
    B. arrives Sunday. Since you'll be in
    C. the Labor Day parade, we could ask Mr.
    D. Krohn, who has a big car, to meet them."

    31.____

32. A. The plumber emerged from the basement and
    B. said, "Mr. Cohen I found the trouble in
    C. your water heater. Could you move those
    D. Schwinn bikes out of my way?"

    32.____

33. A. The President walked slowly to the
    B. podium, bowed to Edward Everett Hale
    C. the other speaker, and began his formal address:
    D. "Fourscore and seven years ago...."

    33.____

34. A. Mr. Fontana, I hope, will arrive before
    B. the beginning of the ceremonies; however,
    C. if his plane is delayed, I have a substitute
    D. speaker who can be here at a moments' notice.

    34.____

35. A. Gladys wedding dress, a satin creation,
     B. lay crumpled on the floor; her veil,
     C. torn and streaked, lay nearby. "Jilted!"
     D. shrieked Gladys. She was clearly annoyed.

36. A. Although it is poor grammar, the word
     B. hopefully has become television's newest
     C. pet expression; I hope (to use the correct
     D. form) that it will soon pass from favor.

37. A.   Plaza Apartment Hotel
     B.   103 Tower road
     C.   Hampstead, Iowa 52025
     D.   March 13, 2021

38. A. Circulation Department
     B. British History Illustrated
     C. 3000 Walnut Street
     D. Boulder Colorado 80302

39. A. Dear Sirs:
     B. Last spring I ordered a subscription to your
     C. magazine. I had read and enjoyed the May
     D. issue containing the article titled "kings."

40. A. I have not however, received a
     B. single issue. Will you check this?
     C. Sincerely,
     D. Maria Herrera

Questions 41-70.

DIRECTIONS: Questions 41 through 70 represent common grammatical concerns: subject-verb agreement, appropriate use of pronouns, and appropriate use of verbs. Read each sentence and indicate the letter of the grammatically CORRECT answer in the space at the right.

41. THE REIVERS, one of William Faulkner's last works, _____ made into a movie starring Steve McQueen.
    A. has been   B. have been   C. are being   D. were

42. He _____ on the ground, his eyes fastened on an ant slowly pushing a morsel of food toward the ant hill.
    A. layed   B. laid   C. had laid   D. lay

43. Nobody in the tri-cities _____ to admit that a flood could be disastrous.
    A. are willing   B. have been willing
    C. is willing   D. were willing

44. "_____," the senator asked, "have you convinced to run against the incumbent?"
    A. Who B. Whom C. Whomever D. Womsoever

45. Of all the psychology courses that I took, Statistics 101 _____ the most demanding.
    A. was B. are C. is D. were

46. Neither the conductor nor the orchestra members _____ the music to be applauded so enthusiastically.
    A. were expecting
    B. was expecting
    C. is expected
    D. has been expecting

47. The requirements for admission to the Lettermen's Club _____ posted outside the athletic director's office for months.
    A. was B. was being C. has been D. have been

48. Please give me a list of the people _____ to compete in the kayak race.
    A. whom you think have planned
    B. who you think has planned
    C. who you think is planning
    D. who you think are planning

49. I saw Eloise and Abelard earlier today; _____ were riding around in a fancy 1956 MG.
    A. she and him B. her and him C. she and he D. her and he

50. If you _____ the trunk in the attic, I'll unpack it later today.
    A. can sit
    B. are able to sit
    C. can set
    D. have sat

51. _____ all of the flour been used, or may I borrow three cups?
    A. Have B. Has C. Is D. Could

52. In exasperation, the cycle shop's owner suggested that _____ there too long.
    A. us boys were
    B. we boys were
    C. us boys had been
    D. we boys had been

53. Idleness as well as money _____ the root of all evil.
    A. have been
    B. were to have been
    C. is
    D. are

54. Only the string players from the quartet—Gregory, Isaac, _____—remained after the concert to answer questions.
    A. him, and I
    B. he, and I
    C. him, and me
    D. he, and me

55. Of all the antiques that _____ for sale, Gertrude chose to buy a stupid glass thimble.
    A. was
    B. is
    C. would have
    D. were

56. The detective snapped, "Don't confuse me with theories about _____ you believe committed the crime!"
    A. who   B. whom   C. whomever   D. which

57. _____ when we first called, we might have avoided our present predicament.
    A. The plumber's coming   B. If the plumber would have come
    C. If the plumber had come   D. If the plumber was to have come

58. We thought the sun _____ in the north until we discovered that our compass was defective.
    A. had rose   B. had risen
    C. had rised   D. had raised

59. Each play of Shakespeare's _____ more than _____ share of memorable characters.
    A. contain its   B. contains; its
    C. contains; it's   D. contain; their

60. Our English teacher suggested to _____ seniors that either Tolstoy or Dickens _____ the outstanding novelist of the nineteenth century.
    A. we; was considered   B. we; were considered
    C. us; was considered   D. us; were considered

61. Sherlock Holmes, together with his great friend and companion Dr. Watson, _____ to aid the woman _____ had stumbled into the room.
    A. has agreed; who   B. have agreed; whom
    C. has agreed; whom   D. have agreed; who

62. Several of the deer _____ when they spotted my backpack _____ open in the meadow.
    A. was frightened; laying   B. were frightened; lying
    C. were frightened; laying   D. was frightened; lying

63. After the Scholarship Committee announces _____ selection, hysterics often _____.
    A. it's; occur   B. its; occur
    C. their; occur   D. their; occurs

64. I _____ the key on the table last night so you and _____ could find it.
    A. layed; her   B. lay; she
    C. laid; she   D. laid; her

65. Some of the antelope _____ wandered away from the meadow where the rancher _____ the block of salt.
    A. has; sat   B. has; set
    C. have; had set   D. has; sets

66. Macaroni and cheese _____ best to us (that is, to Andy and _____) when Mother adds extra cheddar cheese.
    A. tastes; I
    B. tastes; me
    C. taste; me
    D. taste; I

67. Frank said, "It must have been _____ called the phone company."
    A. she who
    B. she whom
    C. her who
    D. her whom

68. The herd _____ moving restlessly at every bolt of lightning; it was either Ted or _____ who saw the beginning of the stampede.
    A. was; me
    B. were; I
    C. was; I
    D. have been; me

69. The foreman _____ his lateness by saying that his alarm clock _____ until six minutes before eight.
    A. explains; had not rang
    B. explained; has not rung
    C. has explained; rung
    D. explained; hadn't rung

70. Of all the coaches, Ms. Cox is the only one who _____ that Sherry dives more gracefully than _____.
    A. is always saying; I
    B. is always saying; me
    C. are always saying; I
    D. were always saying; me

Questions 71-90.

DIRECTIONS: Choose the word in Questions 71 through 90 that is MOST opposite in meaning to the italicized word.

71. *fact*
    A. statistic
    B. statement
    C. incredible
    D. conjecture

72. *stiff*
    A. fastidious
    B. babble
    C. supple
    D. apprehensive

73. *blunt*
    A. concise
    B. tactful
    C. artistic
    D. humble

74. *foreign*
    A. pertinent
    B. comely
    C. strange
    D. scrupulous

75. *anger*
    A. infer
    B. pacify
    C. taint
    D. revile

76. *frank*
    A. earnest
    B. reticent
    C. post
    D. expensive

77. *secure*
 A. precarious B. acquire C. moderate D. frenzied

78. *petty*
 A. harmonious B. careful
 C. forthright D. momentous

79. *concede*
 A. dispute B. reciprocate
 C. subvert D. propagate

80. *benefit*
 A. liquidation B. bazaar
 C. detriment D. profit

81. *capricious*
 A. preposterous B. constant
 C. diabolical D. careless

82. *boisterous*
 A. devious B. valiant C. girlish D. taciturn

83. *harmony*
 A. congruence B. discord C. chagrin D. melody

84. *laudable*
 A. auspicious B. despicable
 C. acclaimed D. doubtful

85. *adherent*
 A. partisan B. stoic C. renegade D. recluse

86. *exuberant*
 A. frail B. corpulent C. austere D. bigot

87. *spurn*
 A. accede B. flail C. efface D. annihilate

88. *spontaneous*
 A. hapless B. corrosive
 C. intentional D. willful

89. *disparage*
 A. abolish B. exude C. incriminate D. extol

90. *timorous*
 A. succinct B. chaste C. audacious D. insouciant

KEY (CORRECT ANSWERS)

1. D	21. A	41. A	61. A	81. B
2. C	22. B	42. D	62.	82. D
3. B	23. C	43. C	63. B	83. B
4. C	24. B	44. B	64. C	84. B
5. C	25. C	45. A	65. C	85. C
6. C	26. C	46. A	66. B	86. C
7. B	27. D	47. D	67. A	87. A
8. B	28. B	48. A	68. C	88. C
9. A	29. B	49. C	69. D	89. D
10. C	30. C	50. C	70. A	90. C
11. C	31. A	51. B	71. D	
12. D	32. B	52. D	72. C	
13. C	33. B	53. C	73. B	
14. C	34. D	54. B	74. A	
15. A	35. A	55. D	75. B	
16. C	36. B	56. B	76. B	
17. A	37. B	57. C	77. A	
18. D	38. D	58. B	78. D	
19. B	39. D	59. B	79. A	
20. B	40. A	60. C	80. C	

EXAMINATION SECTION
TEST 1

DIRECTIONS: Each question or incomplete statement is followed by several suggested answers or completions. Select the one that BEST answers the question or completes the statement. *PRINT THE LETTER OF THE CORRECT ANSWER IN THE SPACE AT THE RIGHT.*

Questions 1-16.

DIRECTIONS: Each sentence below has one or two blanks, each blank indicating that something has been omitted. Beneath the sentence are five words or sets of words labeled A through E. Choose the word or set of words that, when inserted in the sentence, BEST fits the meaning of the sentence as a whole.

Example:
Medieval kingdoms did not become constitutional republics overnight; on the contrary, the change was _____.
   A. unpopular   B. unexpected
   C. advantageous   D. sufficient
   E. gradual

The CORRECT answer is E.

1. The audience responded enthusiastically to Wynton Marsalis' performance of Duke Ellington's music; some of the pieces were interrupted by _____.
   A. melodies   B. interpretations   C. insinuations
   D. assertions   E. applause

1._____

2. People often learn more effectively when studying in groups, and many report that they enjoy these cooperative ventures more than _____ sessions.
   A. temporary   B. solitary   C. collective
   D. unscheduled   E. curtailed

2._____

3. Although Russians rank this poet among their _____ authors, his works have not been _____ in translation.
   A. strangest; understood   B. greatest; appreciated
   C. wittiest; neglected   D. dullest; enjoyed
   E. firmest; altered

3._____

4. The annual summer _____ of the ice sheet covering that part of the sea provides _____ for marine creatures because it releases into the water the algae community that had been trapped in the ice.
   A. drifting; warmth   B. growth; fodder
   C. thinning; light   D. shifting; space
   E. melting; food

4._____

5. Lead in paint and in gasoline has been found to be such an environmental hazard that its use is now
   A. condoned   B. insufficient   C. restricted
   D. rampant   E. unmonitored

6. Astronomy is no longer _____ the shortcomings of human vision; it now benefits from instruments that can see throughout a much broader spectrum.
   A. independent of   B. ambivalent toward
   C. limited by   D. knowledgeable about
   E. fixated on

7. The introductory essay was a(n) _____ effort in that each of the three editors wrote the portion concerning her own field of expertise.
   A. collaborative   B. disagreeable   C. indisputable
   D. enduring   E. unrealistic

8. Texas author Larry McMurtry suggests that those who _____ the moral character of cowboys have been seduced by the idea that a rugged, _____ way of life is less corrupting than the life cities have to offer.
   A. understand; reprobate   B. slander; unfettered
   C. ignore; sinister   D. romanticize; political
   E. idealize; rural

9. Margaret Mead studied ways that some non-Western societies deal effectively with certain human experiences and suggested that such strategies might offer remedies for _____ in American responses to similar events.
   A. ideals   B. assumptions   C. idiosyncrasies
   D. shortcomings   E. improvisations

10. Goya's success as a painter for the Spanish court was _____, for the royal family continued to give him its patronage while he produced art that was widely interpreted as an indictment of monarchical rule.
    A. paradoxical   B. quixotic   C. auspicious
    D. exemplary   E. unfulfilled

11. A short-term pessimist but a long-term optimist, she predicts _____ transition from an epoch of competition to one of _____.
    A. an instantaneous; leisure   B. a retrograde; affluence
    C. an insidious; terror   D. a turbulent; fraternity
    E. a beneficent; militarism

12. The _____ the conflict unleashed in the nation's people have made it impossible for them, even decades later, to discuss the subject with _____.
    A. passions; equanimity   B. fears; trepidation
    C. hatreds; anger   D. visions; honor
    E. emotions; hesitation

13. The _____ of the service sector in our country disturbs many who believe that service industries are of less _____ than manufacturing in promoting economic well-being.
    A. productivity; versatility
    B. balance; volatility
    C. burgeoning; value
    D. contribution; interest
    E. decline; significance

13.____

14. The award-winning design of this solar-heated house has an _____ value over and above the _____ value it possesses due to the rise in the price of fossil fuels.
    A. accessible; unwarranted
    B. ostentatious; superficial
    C. ephemeral; ecological
    D. ornamental; artistic
    E. aesthetic; pragmatic

14.____

15. Giant pandas tend to move _____; they have little need for speed.
    A. implacably
    B. spontaneously
    C. dexterously
    D. deliberately
    E. resoundingly

15.____

16. Helga gave orders in such a _____ way that it was clear the expected people to obey her immediately.
    A. peremptory
    B. timorous
    C. garrulous
    D. facetious
    E. redundant

16.____

Questions 17-22.

DIRECTIONS: Questions 17 through 22 are to be answered on the basis of the following passage, which is adapted from a survey of two hundred years of Hispanic theater in the Southwest.

The majority of the plays produced in the Hispanic theater in the southwestern United States during the early decades of the twentieth century were examples of the plays typically produced in the major cities of Mexico and Spain. Playwrights and impresarios did not hesitate to deal with controversial material. Many of their plays dealt
(5)   with the historical and current circumstances of Hispanic people in the Southwest, but always with the seriousness and propriety.
      Also produced, however, were *revistas*. The *revistas* was a genre that specialized in piquant political satire and commentary: it was a forum for articulating grievances, for poking fun at the governments of both Mexico and the United States, for satirically
(10) considering the Mexican Revolution, and for contrasting Mexican-American culture with Mexican culture. This social and political commentary was carried out despite the fact that both audiences and performers were mostly immigrants who felt themselves liable to deportation or repatriation.
      It should be emphasized that, from the beginning of the Hispanic theater in the
(15) Southwest, the relationship of performers and theaters with the community was close. The Hispanic theater served to reinforce the sense of community by bringing all Spanish speakers together in a cultural act: the preservation and support of the language and art of Mexican people and other Hispanic people in the face of the threat of domination from Anglo-American culture. Theater, more than any other art form, became essential to
(20) promoting ethnic and national identification and to solidifying the colony of expatriates.

Thus, in addition to its artistic functions within the expatriate Mexican community, theater took on specific social functions that were not widely assumed by theaters in Mexico and Spain.

(25) The professional theater houses became temples of culture where the Hispanic community as a whole, regardless of social class, religion, or region of origin, could gather and, in the words of a theater critic writing in 1930, *keep the lamp of our culture lighted.* In 1916 a drama critic for San Antonio's LA PRENSA underlined the social and nationalistic functions of the theater: *Attending the artistic performances at the Teatro Juarez can be considered a patriotic deed which assists in cultural solidarity in support*
(30) *of a modest group of Mexican actors who are fighting for their livelihood in a foreign land and who introduce us to the most precious jewels of contemporary theater in our native tongue that is, the sweet and sonorous language of Cervantes.* Thus, the Hispanic theater became an institution in the Southwest for the preservation of the Hispanic culture and the Spanish language of the dominant Anglo-American society.

17. The passage is PRIMARILY concerned with the
    A. differences among various kinds of plays produced in the Southwest
    B. social and political function of the Hispanic theater in the Southwest
    C. relationship between Mexican theater and the theater of the Southwest
    D. celebration of theater as an important art form
    E. political views of Hispanic actors and playwrights

18. The author gives the MOST emphasis to which of the following aspects of the Hispanic theater?
    The
    A. theater's superiority to other art forms
    B. importance of satirical plays
    C. theater's difference from theater in Mexico and Spain
    D. economic situation of actors and producers
    E. theater's role in building a sense of community

19. Which of the following BEST describes the author's attitude toward those who participated in performances of *revistas*?
    A. Criticism of their lack of seriousness
    B. Mild criticism of their attitude toward government
    C. Admiration for the understatement of their political commentary
    D. Admiration for the subtlety of their art
    E. Respect for their determination

20. By quoting LA PRENSA's drama critic (lines 28-32), the author of the passage PRIMARILY intends to
    A. demonstrate the financial plight of expatriate actors
    B. show appreciation for great artistic performances
    C. praise the translation done for the Hispanic theater
    D. draw attention to the influence of Cervantes
    E. emphasize the role of theater in establishing cultural unity

21. Which of the following can be inferred from the remarks of LA PRENSA's drama critic about the performances at the Teatro Juarez (lines 28-32)?
    The
    A. actors were not willing to boast about their talents
    B. critic recently had seen a play that dealt with matters of wealth and poverty
    C. language used in the productions did not meet the critic's approval
    D. actors were in a precarious economic situation
    E. performance was taking place during a time of intense military conflict

21.____

22. In the final statement in the passage, the author suggests that
    A. only professional theatrical institutions can preserve Hispanic culture
    B. only the theater can preserve culture in a foreign environment
    C. Hispanic people used the theater as an instrument of economic opportunity
    D. preserving Hispanic culture was important in a non-Hispanic political environment
    E. theater was the least understood of all southwestern art forms

22.____

Questions 23-29.

DIRECTIONS: Questions 23 through 29 are to be answered on the basis of the following passages, which discuss the relationship between people and technology in modern society.

Passage 1

Anti-technologists treat technology as something that has escaped from human control. In the face of today's excruciatingly complex problems, it is understandable that many people agree with them. When people engage in technological activities, these activities appear to have consequences, not only physical but also intellectual,
(5) psychological, and cultural. Thus, anti-technologists argue, technology is deterministic. It causes other things to happen. Someone invents the automobile, for example, and it changes the way people think as well as the way they act. It changes their living patterns, their values, and their expectations in ways that were not anticipated when the automobile was first introduced. Some of the changes appear to be not only
(10) unanticipated but undesired. Nobody wanted traffic jams, accidents, and pollution. Therefore, technological advance seems to be independent of human direction. But sober thought reveals that technology is not an independent force, much less a thing, but one of the types of activities in which people engage.

The anti-technologists discount completely the integrity and intelligence of the
(15) ordinary person. Indeed, pity and disdain for the individual citizen are essential aspects of anti-technology. One of its dogmas is that technological society forces people to consume things that they do not really desire. How can we respond to this falsehood? One might observe that the consumers who buy cars and electric can openers could, if they chose, buy oboes and oil paints, sailboats, and hiking boots, chess sets and
(20) recordings of Mozart. Or, could they not help purchase a kidney machine that would save their neighbor's life? If people are vulgar, foolish, and selfish in their choice of purchases, is it not the worst sort of excuse to blame this on technological society?

Indeed, wouldn't people prefer being called vulgar to being told that they have no will with which to make choices of their own?

Passage 2

(25) A happy technologist once asserted that everyone lampoons modern technology but no one is prepared to give up his or her refrigerator. In the United States there is a general perception that life-style, or the way in which one lives, is a matter of individual choice, at least for a vast majority. Disregarding economic means for a moment, people think that one can choose to lead either a bohemian life-style or a conventional one. But is one truly free to choose to have a refrigerator or not? Is it a simple matter of life-style choice or do other institutional arrangements of society impinge with demands of their
(30) own?

A refrigerator (including freezer) performs several functions. It stores food (a necessity) and cools drinks or produces ice for cooling drinks (a comfort or luxury). The latter category is not an essential function. The desirability of cold beer, for example, is culturally or socially induced; other cultures find warm beer more desirable, so people in
(35) those societies do not need a refrigerator to perform this particular function. Consider another society in which it is possible for people to purchase their perishable food on a daily basis in markets or small shops, easily accessible and within walking distance of their homes. This option is not available to many people in the United States. The supermarket as a social institution, not within walking distance of most people, has its
(40) own imperatives. One buys for a week of eating, not for a day, so storage in a refrigerator becomes essential to living. It is a necessity induced by a life-style over which individuals have little control. To chide individuals for recalcitrance or perversity for their unwillingness to give up their refrigerators is to misjudge profoundly the nature of contemporary technology and its induced social change. It is irrelevant to the
(45) argument whether or not a supermarket/refrigerator society has advantages over the other.

The only question is, do individuals have autonomy to choose freely one or the other?

23. In Passage 1, the author's attitude toward anti-technologists is BEST described as
    A. sympathetic   B. indifferent   C. amused
    D. fearful   E. critical

24. In line 12, *sober* MOST NEARLY means
    A. plain and uncomplicated   B. not intoxicated
    C. sensible   D. unimaginative
    E. alert

25. The author uses the word *dogmas* (line 16) to refer to what he considers to be
    A. religious truths   B. logical premises
    C. prophetic ideas   D. unassailable doctrines
    E. groundless assumptions

26. The author of Passage 2 argues that in much of the United States a refrigerator is an
    A. appliance that has both essential and culturally determined functions
    B. example of modern technology that allows individuals to pursue different life-styles
    C. invention that only recently has become affordable
    D. entity that is independent of a social institution such as the supermarket
    E. illustration of the mindless materialism of modern society

27. What would be the likely response of the author of Passage 2 to the discussion of cars in lines 8-13 of Passage 1?
    A. Consumers have a wide variety of cars from which to choose.
    B. Consumers in some areas must rely on cars for transportation.
    C. Consumers tend to perceive cars as a means of recreation.
    D. Cars are not as essential as refrigerators or medical equipment in most societies.
    E. Cars as possessions are overvalued in modern society.

28. Which BEST describes an assumption about people held by the authors of Passages 1 and 2?
    A. People themselves are to blame for problems in modern society.
    B. People should not be judged too hastily about the choices they make.
    C. The author of Passage 1 views people as reasonable, whereas the author of Passage 2 views the as unreasonable.
    D. The author of Passage 1 views people as altruistic, whereas the author of Passage 2 views them as selfish.
    E. The author of Passage 1 views all people as essentially honest, whereas the author of Passage 2 thinks that only a few are.

29. The author of Passage 1 and the author of Passage 2 DISAGREE most strongly about the
    A. value of particular products of modern technology
    B. seriousness of problems associated with modern technology
    C. availability of consumer goods in a modern technological society
    D. control that people have over the uses and effects of technology
    E. type of life-style enjoyed by the majority of people in a modern technological society

Questions 30-41.

DIRECTIONS: Each question below consists of a related pair of words or phrases, followed by five pairs of words or phrases labeled A through E. Select the pair that BEST expresses a relationship similar to that expressed in the original pair.

        Example: CRUMB : BREAD
          A. ounce : unit   B. splinter : wood
          C. water : bucket   D. twine : rope
          E. cream : butter

The CORRECT answer is B.

30. WRITE : SCRIBBLE
    A. hear : mumble   B. draw : doodle   C. study : concentrate
    D. plan : design   E. read : learn

31. MICROSCOPE : SMALL
    A. kilometer : metric   B. thermometer : hot
    C. telescope : distant   D. stethoscope : loud
    E. calculator : fast

32. CALLIGRAPHER : PAPER
    A. plumber : wrench   B. potter : kiln
    C. prospector : ore   D. painter : canvas
    E. printer : ink

33. WHIFF : NOSE
    A. applause : hands   B. lick : cat
    C. pout : lips   D. spark : fire
    E. glimpse : eyes

34. MANUAL : INSTRUCTIONS
    A. timetable : railroads   B. food : utensils
    C. bibliography : sources   D. magazine : subscriptions
    E. radio : listeners

35. ITINERARY : TRIP
    A. schedule : table   B. agenda : meeting
    C. amendment : document   D. diary : experience
    E. memorandum : record

36. ACROBAT : TRAPEZE
    A. boxer : ring   B. actor : role
    C. swimmer : lap   D. animal : cage
    E. vaulter : pole

37. MISNOMER : NAME
    A. error : mishap   B. variability
    C. exception : rule   D. misconception : idea
    E. misdeed : apology

38. RECONCILE : HARMONY
    A. cure : health   B. disturb : tranquility
    C. perform : entertainment   D. forecast : weather

39. PARABLE : ILLUSTRATIVE
    A. newspaper : daily   B. joke : amusing
    C. cliche : creative   D. lecture : spoken
    E. film : exposed

40. RAMBLE : DIGRESSIVE
    A. warn : protected
    B. prattle : foolish
    C. praise : incorrect
    D. whisper : audible
    E. babble : intelligible

41. LURK : FURTIVE
    A. threaten : menacing
    B. accuse : guilty
    C. misrepresent : understated
    D. respect : contemptuous
    E. spy : informative

Questions 42-52.

DIRECTIONS: Questions 42 through 52 are to be answered on the basis of the following passage. Scientists are often considered to be objective, but we are reminded in this passage that scientists are just as much products of their own cultural prejudices as are other people. For example, despite the efforts of early anatomists to represent the body accurately, early anatomical reproductions reflected the stereotypes of the eighteenth and nineteenth centuries: that physical and intellectual strength defined masculinity and motherhood defined femininity.

(5) In 1734 anatomist Bernard Albinus produced an illustration of the male human skeleton that would serve as the model for anatomical illustration for more than 75 years. Albinus consciously sought to capture the details not of a particular body but of a universal and ideal type. Though Albinus' fame rested on his reputation for accuracy, at every step along the way he sacrificed objectivity to the ideal. Having made precise measurements of his subject and transferred them exactly to paper, Albinus then eliminated anatomical details from his drawing that would have destroyed its symmetry.

(10) Having produced the perfect drawing of the male, Albinus lamented, *we lack a female skeleton*. And numerous drawings of female skeletons were made in subsequent years. But, although these drawings purported too represent the female skeleton, they differed greatly from one another.

(15) Marie Thiroux d'Arconville's rendering of a distinctively female skeleton, published in 1759, captured the imagination of physicians for more than half a century. This illustration —one of the very few drawn by a woman anatomist—might also be called the most *sexist* portrayal of a female skeleton. Thiroux d'Arconville exaggerated, almost to the point of caricature, those parts of the body that were emerging as sites of political debate: the skull as a mark of intelligence and the pelvis as a measure of womanliness. She depicted the female skull (incorrectly) as smaller in proportion to the body than the man's. She also focused attention on the pelvis by exaggerating the narrowness of the

(20) ribs so that the pelvis appeared excessively large. It would seem that either Thiroux d'Arconville intended to emphasize narrow ribs and wide hips as a mark of femininity or she chose for her model a woman who had worn a corset throughout her life. As early as 1741, anatomist J.B. Winslow had noted that regular use of the corset deforms the ribs.

(25) In 1796 the German anatomist Samuel Thomas von Soemmerring produced a rival female skeleton. He had spent years perfecting the illustration; when it was finished, he considered it to be of such *completeness* and *exactitude* that it made a perfect mate for the great Albinus male. As a model he selected the skeleton of a twenty-year-old

woman who had borne a child. For proportions, he checked his drawing against
(30) classical statues of Venus. Von Soemmerring intended his skeleton to represent not an individual woman but (as a later commentator put it) *the most beautiful* woman as was imagined to exist in life.

Although Thiroux d'Arconville and von Soemmerring drew their female skeletons from nature and considered their work *exact*, great debate erupted over the precise
(35) features of the female skeleton. In contrast to Thiroux d'Arconville, von Soemmerring portrayed the skull of the female (correctly) as larger in proportion to the body than that of the male. He drew the ribs smaller in proportion to the hips than the man's, but not remarkably so.

Despite (or perhaps because of) its exaggerations, the Thiroux d'Arconville skeleton
(40) became the favored drawing. Von Soemmerring's skeleton, by contrast, was attacked for its *inaccuracies*. Edinburgh physician John Barclay criticized von Soemmerring in particular for showing the incorrect proportion of the ribs to the hips; he argued that the female rib cage is much smaller than that shown by von Soemmerring because women's restricted life-style required that they breathe less vigorously. Barclay concluded that
(45) von Soemmerring was an artist, but no anatomist.

Rejecting Thiroux d'Arconville's insistence that the female skull was smaller in proportion to the body than the male skull, von Soemmerring pointed out that women's skulls are actually heavier than men's, relative to total body weight (1:6 for women, 1:8 to 1:10 for men).
(50) Von Soemmerring's view was castigated, for it seemed to counter the idea that men were the more intelligent and creative of the species. In subsequent years, however, anatomists had to concede the truth of von Soemmerring's depiction of the female skull. Yet they did not conclude that women's large skulls were loaded with heavy, high-powered brains. Rather than a mark of intelligence, women's large skulls were
(55) dismissed as a sign of incomplete development. John Barclay, for example, used the proportionally larger size of the female skull to support that physiologically women resemble children, whose skulls are also large relative to their body size.

42. The PRIMARY focus of the passage is on
   A. the effects of Albinus' pioneering work in human anatomy
   B. the influence of social ideas or scientific thinking
   C. conflicting definitions of the ideal male skeleton
   D. the changes in cultural values brought about by the study of anatomy
   E. how similar the male and female skeletons really are

43. According to the passage, Albinus misrepresented certain bone structures in order to
   A. enhance individual variations in the models he used
   B. make structural details more readily visible
   C. make the skeleton conform to his idea of aesthetic perfection
   D. surpass all previous anatomists in exactness
   E. emphasize differences between male and female skeletons

44. In line 10, *the* is underlined in order to indicate that
    A. artistic tastes were changing rapidly during this period
    B. the author is referring to a particular and very important drawing of a woman
    C. there was a great deal of similarity among the drawings mentioned
    D. the drawings were exact representations of the particular models used
    E. each artist intended the drawing to represent an ideal, universal woman

45. The passage supports which of the following statements about Thiroux d'Arconville's drawing?
    It
    A. reflected physicians' superior knowledge of anatomy
    B. set a new standard for precision of detail
    C. was more reliable than drawings by male artists
    D. conformed to prevailing views about femininity
    E. was free of the inaccuracies of the classical era

46. The author MOST likely gives a description of von Soermmerring's human model (lines 35-38) in order to suggest that
    A. motherhood and youth were thought to be characteristics of the ideal woman
    B. Winslow's idea that corsets could be harmful was probably based on inadequate evidence
    C. no ordinary woman's skeleton could measure up to the classical idea of beauty
    D. von Soemmerring's powers of observation were superior to those of his critics
    E. von Soemmerring's ideas about skull size were affected by the youthfulness of his model

47. In line 34, *erupted* MOST NEARLY means
    A. ejected
    B. overflowed
    C. increased
    D. broke out
    E. became uncontrollable

48. The author uses the parenthetical phrase *or perhaps because of* in line 39 in order to suggest that
    A. Thiroux d'Arconville's contemporaries tended to share her prejudices
    B. exaggerated drawings are often more useful for conveying fine details
    C. artistic tastes of the eighteenth century regarded exaggeration as beautiful
    D. the author is uncertain about the causes of the drawing's popularity
    E. Thiroux d'Arconville was never fully understood by either the artists or the scientists of her day

49. The passage implies that von Soemmerring's chief reason for drawing the female skull proportionally larger than the male skull was his wish to
    A. reflect actual physical evidence
    B. correct the distortions in Albinus' work
    C. disprove Barclay's ideas
    D. suggest that women were more intelligent than men
    E. create an aesthetically pleasing work of art

50. The discussion in lines 42-44 about the size of the female rib cage CHIEFLY serves to
    A. show that scientists were concerned with both aesthetics and facts
    B. lead the reader to realize that neither Thiroux d'Arconville's nor von Soemmerring's drawings were entirely accurate
    C. indicate the bias held by most scientists of the period by citing a representative view
    D. contrast with the remarks about female beauty made by the *later commentator* (line 31)
    E. present evidence in support of von Soemmerring's position in the debate

51. Barclay's appraisal of von Soemmerring (lines 43-45) was intended to
    A. praise his skill as a draftsman
    B. emphasize the beauty of his drawing
    C. criticize the excessive embellishment of his drawing
    D. cast doubt on the scientific accuracy of his drawing
    E. suggest that creativity is an important factor in science

52. In line 52, *concede* MOST NEARLY means
    A. acknowledge   B. compromise   C. renounce
    D. disclose   E. surrender

Questions 53-60.

DIRECTIONS: Questions 53 through 60 are too be answered on the basis of the following passage, which is adapted from an American writer's memoir of his childhood.

My father taught me skills and manners: he taught me to shoot, to drive fast, to read respectfully, too handle a boat, and to distinguish between good jazz music and bad. His codes were not novel, but they were rigid. A gentleman was a stickler for precision; life was no more than an inventory of small choices that together formed a man's
(5)   character, entire.
He looked, and spoke, straight at you. He could stare down anyone. To me everything about him seemed outsized. Doing a school report on the Easter Islanders I found in an encyclopedia pictures of their huge sculptures, and there he was, massive head and nose, nothing subtle or delicate. He was in fact (and how diminishing those
(10) words, *in fact*, look to me now) an inch or two above six feet, full-bodied, a man who lumbered from here to there with deliberation. When I was a child I noticed that people were respectful of the cubic feet my father occupied; later I understood that I had confused respect with resentment.

　　　　　I remember his shoes, so meticulously selected and cared for and used, thin-soled,
(15)　with cracked uppers, older than I was or could ever be, shining dully and from the
　　　depths. Just a pair of shoes?
　　　　　No: I knew before I knew any other complicated thing that for my father there was
　　　nothing he possessed that I was *just* something. His pocket watch was not *just* a
　　　timepiece, it was a miraculous instrument. It struck the hour unassertively, like a silver
(20)　tine touched to a crystal glass, no hurry, you might like to know it's noon.
　　　　　He despised black leather, said black shoes reminded him of black attache cases, of
　　　bankers, lawyers, look-before-you-leapers anxious not to offend their clients. He owned
　　　nothing black except his umbrella. His umbrella doubled as a shooting stick, and one
　　　afternoon at soccer game he was sitting on it when a man asked him what he would do
(25)　if it rained, sit wet or stand dry? I laughed. My father laughed also, but tightly, and he
　　　did not reply; nor did we ever again use this quixotic contraption. He took things, *things*,
　　　seriously.
　　　　　When I was a boy, he introduced me, with ceremony, to a couple of family treasures:
　　　my great-grandfather's medical degree from Leyden and, set in blue-velvet cavities in a
(30)　worn leather case, my grandfather's surgical instruments. These totems are gone now,
　　　lost during one or another last-minute, dark-of-night escape from a house where the rent
　　　was seven months overdue. Recently I bought a set of compasses and dividers solely
　　　because, snuggled in their own blue-velvet nests, they returned me to evenings when I
　　　sat beside my father and he showed me the probes and scalpels. I would examine a
(35)　piece, then return it to its place, and promise never to touch it without supervision. I was
　　　warned that microbes deadly beyond imagining still lurked on the blades, but there was
　　　no need to scare me away from them. I had never seen things so mysterious, cold, or
　　　menacing.

53. The passage portrays the father as a man who is PRIMARILY
    A. exuberant
    B. malicious
    C. long-winded
    D. complex and preoccupied with appearances
    E. generous and thoughtful toward others

54. The list of skills in the first sentence indicates the father's
    A. self-discipline　　B. lack of subtlety　　C. impatience
    D. practicality　　　E. versatility

55. The author mentions the Easter Island statues (lines 6-10) in order to emphasis his father's apparent
    A. indifference　　B. energy　　C. massiveness
    D. good looks　　 E. stodginess

56. Black leather (lines 21-23) represents which of the following for the father?
    A. Reckless pursuit of goals　　B. Extraordinary self-discipline
    C. Unabashed greed　　　　　 D. Excessive caution
    E. Admirably good manners

57. The incident at the soccer game (lines 24-26) shows that the father
    A. was too depressed to be able to enjoy jokes
    B. was unreasonably fearful of strangers
    C. was extremely sensitive to the judgment of others
    D. was able to compromise when necessary
    E. had an unpredictable and violent temper

58. The passage does all of the following to establish the father's character EXCEPT
    A. describe him physically
    B. quote his words directly
    C. recount the son's youthful attitude toward him
    D. show him interacting with others
    E. comment on his likes and dislikes

59. The writer emphasizes an aspect of his father's character that is in ironic contrast to his outsized and obtrusive appearance, which had *nothing subtle* or *delicate* (line 14) about it.
    This trait of his personality would be
    A. crude sense of humor
    B. animosity towards bankers and lawyers
    C. attention to detail exemplified by his meticulously selected shoes and his musically precise pocket watch
    D. the respect he inspired because of his formidable size
    E. a sentimental attachment to family heirlooms

60. The style and tone of this passage may be described as being predominantly
    A. humorous and sarcastic
    B. poetic and metaphorical
    C. descriptive, reminiscent and nostalgic
    D. factual and pedantic
    E. sharply satiric

KEY (CORRECT ANSWERS)

1.	E	11.	D	21.	D	31.	C	41.	A	51.	D
2.	B	12.	A	22.	D	32.	D	42.	B	52.	A
3.	B	13.	C	23.	E	33.	E	43.	C	53.	D
4.	E	14.	E	24.	C	34.	C	44.	E	54.	E
5.	C	15.	D	25.	E	35.	B	45.	D	55.	C
6.	C	16.	A	26.	A	36.	E	46.	A	56.	D
7.	A	17.	B	27.	B	37.	D	47.	D	57.	C
8.	E	18.	E	28.	B	38.	A	48.	A	58.	B
9.	D	19.	E	29.	D	39.	B	49.	A	59.	C
10.	A	20.	E	30.	B	40.	B	50.	C	60.	C

EXAMINATION SECTION
TEST 1

DIRECTIONS: Each question or incomplete statement is followed by several suggested answers or completions. Select the one that BEST answers the question or completes the statement. *PRINT THE LETTER OF THE CORRECT ANSWER IN THE SPACE AT THE RIGHT.*

Questions 1-50.

DIRECTIONS: One word in each of Questions 1 through 50 is MISSPELLED. Indicate the letter of the MISSPELLED word in the space at the right.

1. A. statute   B. stationary   1._____
   C. staturesque   D. stature

2. A. practicible   B. practical   2._____
   C. particle   D. reticule

3. A. plague   B. plaque   C. ague   D. aigrete   3._____

4. A. theology   B. idealogy   4._____
   C. psychology   D. philology

5. A. dilema   B. stamina   5._____
   C. feminine   C. strychnine

6. A. deceit   B. benefit   C. grieve   D. hienous   6._____

7. A. commensurable B. measurable   7._____
   C. duteable   C. salable

8. A. homogeneous   B. heterogeneous   8._____
   C. advantageous   D. religeous

9. A. criticize   B. dramatise   C. exorcise   D. exercise   9._____

10. A. maintain   B. maintainance   10._____
    C. sustain   D. sustenance

11. A. portend   B. portentious   11._____
    C. pretend   D. pretentious

12. A. prophesize   B. prophesies   12._____
    C. farinaceous   D. spaceous

13. A. choose   B. chose   C. choosen   D. chasten   13._____

14. A. censure   B. censorious   14._____
    C. pleasure   D. pleasurible

15. A. cover   B. coverage   C. adder   D. adege   15._____

16. A. balloon   B. diregible   C. direct   D. descent   16._____

2 (#1)

17.	A. whemsy	B. crazy	C. flimsy	D. lazy	17.____
18.	A. derision	B. pretention			18.____
	C. sustention	D. contention			
19.	A. question	B. questionaire			19.____
	A. legion	B. legionary			
20.	A. chattle	B. cattle	C. dismantle	D. kindle	20.____
21.	A. canal	B. cannel	C. chanel	D. colonel	21.____
22.	A. hemorrage	B. storage	C. manage	D. foliage	22.____
23.	A. surgeon	B. sturgeon	C. luncheon	D. stancheon	23.____
24.	A. facial	B. physical	C. fiscle	D. muscle	24.____
25.	A. congradulate	B. percolate			25.____
	C. major	D. leisure			
26.	A. convenience	B. privilige			26.____
	C. emerge	D. immerse			
27.	A. erasable	B. inflammable			27.____
	C. audable	D. laudable			
28.	A. final	B. fines	C. finis	D. Finish	28.____
29.	A. emitted	B. representative			29.____
	C. discipline	D. insistance			
30.	A. diphthong	B. rarified	C. library	D. recommend	30.____
31.	A. compel	B. belligerent			31.____
	C. successful	D. sargeant			
32.	A. dispatch	B. dispise	C. dispose	D. dispute	32.____
33.	A. administrator	B. adviser			33.____
	C. diner	D. celluler			
34.	A. ignite	B. ignision	C. igneous	D. ignited	34.____
35.	A. pallor	B. ballid	C. ballet	D. pallid	35.____
36.	A. urbane	B. surburbane			36.____
	C. interurban	D. urban			
37.	A. symtom	B. serum			37.____
	C. antiseptic	D. aromatic			
38.	A. register	B. registrar	C. purser	D. burser	38.____
39.	A. athletic	B. tragedy			39.____
	C. batallion	D. sophomore			

3 (#1)

40. A. latent B. godess C. aisle D. whose 40.____
41. A. rhyme B. rhythm C. thime D. thine 41.____
42. A. eighth B. exaggerate 42.____
    C. electoral D. villain
43. A. statute B. superintendent 43.____
    C. iresistible D. colleague
44. A. sieze B. therefor C. auxiliary D. changeable 44.____
45. A. siege B. knowledge 45.____
    C. lieutenent D. weird
46. A. acquitted B. polititian 46.____
    C. professor D. conqueror
47. A. changeable B. chargeable 47.____
    C. salable D. useable
48. A. promissory B. prisoner 48.____
    C. excellent D. tyrrany
49. A. comptroller B. traveled 49.____
    C. accede D. procede
50. A. Britain B. Brittainica 50.____
    C. conductor D. vendor

KEY (CORRECT ANSWERS)

1. C	11. B	21. C	31. D	41. C
2. A	12. D	22. A	32. B	42. C
3. D	13. C	23. D	33. D	43. C
4. B	14. D	24. C	34. B	44. A
5. A	15. D	25. A	35. B	45. C
6. D	16. B	26. B	36. B	46. B
7. C	17. A	27. C	37. A	47. D
8. D	18. B	28. D	38. D	48. D
9. B	19. B	29. D	39. C	49. D
10. B	20. A	30. B	40. B	50. B

CORRECT SPELLING

1. statuesque
2. practicable
3. aigrette
4. ideology
5. dilemma
6. heinous
7. dutiable
8. religious
9. dramatize
10. maintenance
11. portentous
12. spacious
13. chosen
14. pleasurable
15. adage
16. dirigible
17. whimsey or whimsy
18. pretension
19. questionnaire
20. chattel
21. channel
22. hemorrhage
23. stanchion
24. fiscal
25. congratulate
26. privilege
27. audible
28. Finnish
29. insistence
30. rarefied
31. sergeant
32. despise
33. cellular
34. ignition
35. ballad
36. suburban
37. symptom
38. bursar
39. battalion
40. goddess
41. thyme
42. electoral
43. irresistible
44. seize
45. lieutenant
46. politician
47. usable
48. tyranny
49. proceed
50. Britannica

TEST 2

Questions 1-50.

DIRECTIONS: Select the letter of the word or expression that MOST NEARLY expresses the meaning of the capitalized word in the group.

1. FICTITIOUS
   A. turbulent   B. anxious   C. assumed   D. scanty

2. ARDENT
   A. fervid   B. gay   C. savage   D. untamed

3. BLATANT
   A. insipid   B. open   C. closed   D. clamorous

4. DISTRAIT
   A. crooked   B. narrow
   C. broken   D. absentminded

5. EQUITABLE
   A. unbiased   B. unjust
   C. unreasonable   D. unfair

6. EXPEDITE
   A. hinder   B. harm   C. send   D. hasten

7. LUCRATIVE
   A. painful   B. creditable
   C. preferential   D. profitable

8. POSTDATED
   A. past date   B. future date
   C. no date   D. current date

9. RESOURCES
   A. debts   B. liabilities
   C. funds   D. losses

10. AGENDA
    A. receipt   B. agent
    C. combination   D. memoranda

11. DISCRETE
    A. careful   B. prudent   C. truthful   D. separate

12. DOGMATIC
    A. bovine   B. canine   C. opinionated   D. unprincipled

83

13. INTREPID
    A. fearful   B. fearless   C. fanciful   D. cowardly

14. TENACITY
    A. firmness   B. sagacity   C. temerity   D. thinness

15. ASEPTIC
    A. antique   B. artistic   C. sterile   D. austere

16. CREDIBLE
    A. believable   B. unbelievable
    C. correct   D. suitable

17. LESSEE
    A. lender   B. giver   C. receiver   D. renter

18. IGNOMINY
    A. illiteracy   B. ill luck
    C. disgrace   D. despair

19. PRODIGAL
    A. wasteful   B. marvelous   C. ominous   D. harmless

20. VOLUBLE
    A. bulky   B. glib   C. desirable   D. malleable

21. JAMB
    A. doorway   B. crowd   C. fruit   D. animal

22. ATOMIC
    A. combustible   B. minute
    C. crystalline   D. ambient

23. ACUMEN
    A. beauty   B. poise
    C. keen discernment   D. illness

24. SUPERCILIOUS
    A. foolish   B. needless   C. callous   D. haughty

25. SPURIOUS
    A. large   B. small
    C. valid   D. not genuine

26. PREDATORY
    - A. plundering
    - B. fawning
    - C. encouraging
    - D. preceding

27. AMPERSAND
    - A. ammunition
    - B. currency
    - C. abbreviation
    - D. illumination

28. DEHYDRATED
    - A. airless
    - B. worthless
    - C. waterless
    - D. pointless

29. NOCTURNAL
    - A. nightly
    - B. revolving
    - C. daily
    - D. frequently

30. DILATORY
    - A. expanding
    - B. delaying
    - C. watery
    - D. pickling

31. SANGUINE
    - A. baleful
    - B. thirsty
    - C. hopeful
    - D. delinquent

32. PHLEGMATIC
    - A. sluggish
    - B. active
    - C. potent
    - D. secretive

33. PODIATRIST
    - A. head
    - B. infants
    - C. feet
    - D. adults

34. INGENUE
    - A. fashion
    - B. state
    - C. medicine
    - D. stage

35. CORPOREAL
    - A. military
    - B. naval
    - C. bodily
    - D. legal

36. MUNDANE
    - A. stupid
    - B. ladylike
    - C. worldly
    - D. weedy

37. INTERVENE
    - A. induce
    - B. insert
    - C. interfere
    - D. solve

38. IMMINENT
    - A. of high renown
    - B. impending
    - C. very large
    - D. incurable

39. GERMANE
    - A. Teutonic
    - B. relevant
    - C. infectious
    - D. brutal

40. PARITY

    A. doubt
    B. equality
    C. fitness
    D. littleness

41. RATIONALIZE

    A. rattle
    B. explain by reason
    C. limit consumption
    D. charge

42. SUCCINCT

    A. superfluous
    B. concise
    C. ponderous
    D. succulent

43. VENIAL

    A. pardonable
    B. revengeful
    C. fearful
    D. despicable

44. VERBOSITY

    A. bitterness
    B. action
    C. wordiness
    D. speed

45. WITHER

    A. canaries B. cracks C. decay D. trills

46. CIRCUMVENT

    A. outwit B. surround C. open up D. cover

47. COMPLICITY

    A. deceit
    B. delight in society
    C. partnership in wrong
    D. relief from debt

48. IPSO FACTO

    A. by that very fact
    B. made by hand
    C. according to him
    D. as a matter of fact

49. ABSTRUSE

    A. profound B. absurd C. enormous D. ridiculous

50. RESTIVE

    A. permanent B. quiet C. sullen D. impatient

KEY (CORRECT ANSWERS)

1.	C	11.	D	21.	A	31.	C	41.	B
2.	A	12.	C	22.	B	32.	A	42.	B
3.	D	13.	B	23.	C	33.	C	43.	A
4.	D	14.	A	24.	D	34.	D	44.	C
5.	A	15.	C	25.	D	35.	C	45.	C
6.	D	16.	A	26.	A	36.	C	46.	A
7.	D	17.	D	27.	C	37.	C	47.	C
8.	B	18.	C	28.	C	38.	B	48.	A
9.	C	19.	A	29.	A	39.	B	49.	A
10.	D	20.	B	30.	B	40.	B	50.	D

TEST 3

Questions 1-10.

DIRECTIONS: For each word listed below, one correct syllabication is shown. Indicate the CORRECT choice.

1. A. rep er cus sion B. re per cus sion
   C. rep er cuss ion D. re perc us sion

2. A. corr es pon dence B. cor resp on dence
   C. cor re spond ence D. cor res pond ence

3. A. sup er in ten dent B. su per in ten dent
   C. su per int end ent D. su per in tend ent

4. A. ac com mo date B. acc om mod ate
   C. acc omm o date D. ac com mod ate

5. A. ac know ledge B. ac knowl edge
   C. ack nowl edge D. ack now ledge

6. A. aud it or ium B. au dit or ium
   C. aud i tor i um D. au di to ri um

7. A. hosp i tal ize B. hos pit a lize
   C. hosp it al ize D. hos pi tal ize

8. A. du pli ca tion B. dup lic a tion
   C. du plic a tion D. dup li ca tion

9. A. re cap i tu late B. rec ap it u late
   C. re ca pi tu late D. re ca pit u late

10. A. com plim en ta ry B. com pli men ta ry
    C. comp lim ent ar y D. comp li ment a ry

Questions 11-25.

DIRECTIONS: In each of the following groups of sentences, there are three sentences which are correct and one which is incorrect because it contains an error in usage. Indicate the letter of the INCORRECT sentence.

11. A. There was, in the first place, no indication that a crime had been committed.
    B. She is taller than any other member of her class.
    C. She decided to leave the book lay on the table.
    D. Haven't you any film in stock at this time?

12. A. Because they had been trained for emergencies, the assault did not catch them by surprise.
    B. They divided the loot between the four of them in proportion to their effort.
    C. The number of strikes is gradually diminishing.
    D. Between acts we went out to the lobby for a brief chat.

13. A. It is difficult to recollect what life was like before the war.   13.____
    B. Will each of the pupils please hand their home work in?
    C. There are fewer serious mistakes in this pamphlet than I had thought.
    D. "Leave Her to Heaven" is the title of a novel by Ben Ames Williams.

14. A. I was too greatly relieved to be able to say anything.   14.____
    B. These insignia date back to ancient Roman times.
    C. We observed a strange phenomenon; the house seemed to sway in the wind and to tremble like a leaf.
    D. It would be much more preferable if you were no longer seen in his company.

15. A Please send me this data at your earliest convenience.   15.____
    A. The loss of their material proved a severe handicap.
    B. My principal objection to this plan is that it is impracticable.
    C. The doll has lain in the rain all evening.

16. A. I had expected to see my brother.   16.____
    B. He expected to have seen his brother.
    C. I hoped to see you do better.
    D. It was his duty to assist our friend.

17. A. The reason why I am writing to you is that I wish to avoid further misunderstanding.   17.____
    B. These kind of arguments always cause hard feelings.
    C. Regardless of your decision, I shall have to go.
    D. I have only twenty pupils in this class.

18. A. Which is the youngest of the two sisters?   18.____
    B. I am determined to finish the work before Saturday.
    C. It is difficult to see why the problems are not correctly solved.
    D. I have never met a more interesting person.

19. A. Located on a mountainside with a babbling brook beside the door, it was a dream palace.   19.____
    B. Blessed are they that have not seen and yet have believed.
    C. The customs in that part of the country are much different than I expected.
    D. Politics, even in towns of small population, has always attracted ambitious young lawyers.

20. A. Of all my friends he is the one on whom I can most surely depend.   20.____
    B. We value the Constitution because of it's guarantees to freedom.
    C. The audience was deeply stirred by the actor's performance .
    D. Give the book to whoever comes into the room first.

21. A. Everything was in order: the paper ruled, the pencils sharpened, the chairs placed.   21.____
    B. Neither John nor Peter were able to attend the reception.
    C. In April the streets which had been damaged by cold weather were repaired by the workmen.
    D. You may lend my book to the pupil who you think will enjoy it most.

22. A. He fidgeted, like most children do, while the grown-ups were discussing the problem.
    B. I won't go unless you go with me.
    C. Sitting beside the charred ruins of his cabin, the frontiersman told us the story of the attack.
    D. Certainly there can be no objection to the boys" working on a volunteer basis.

23. A. The congregation was dismissed.
    B. The congregation were deeply moved by the sermon.
    C. What kind of an automobile is that?
    D. His explanation and mine agree.

24. A. There is no danger of him being elected.
    B. There is no doubt of his election.
    C. John and he are to be the speakers.
    D. John and she are to be the speakers.

25. A. Them that honor me I will honor.
    B. They that believe in me shall be rewarded.
    C. Who did you see at the meeting?
    D. Whom are you writing to?

KEY (CORRECT ANSWERS)

1.	B		11.	C
2.	C		12.	B
3.	D		13.	B
4.	A		14.	D
5.	B		15.	A
6.	D		16.	B
7.	D		17.	B
8.	A		18.	A
9.	D		19.	C
10.	B		20.	B

21. B
22. A
23. C
24. A
25. C

BASIC MATHEMATICS
EXAMINATION SECTION
TEST 1

DIRECTIONS: Each question or incomplete statement is followed by several suggested answers or completions. Select the one that BEST answers the question or completes the statement. *PRINT THE LETTER OF THE CORRECT ANSWER IN THE SPACE AT THE RIGHT.*

1. Add: 4,898 + 7 + 361 + 26 1.____
   A. 5,282   B. 5,292   C. 5,382   D. 5,392

2. Subtract: 7,006 – 5,797 2.____
   A. 1,209   B. 1,219   C. 1,309   D. 2,209

3. Multiply: 2,759 3.____
   ×806

   A. 234,274   B. 2,173,754   C. 2,174,754   D. 2,223,754

4. Divide: $87\sqrt{72{,}732}$ 4.____
   A. 835   B. 836   C. 846   D. 976

5. Combine: (+6)−(−4)+(−3) 5.____
   A. −1   B. +1   C. +7   D. +13

6. Simplify: [(−7) × (−8)] ÷ (−4) 6.____

7. Add: 1 4/9 + 5 3/4 7.____
   A. 6 7/13   B. 6 7/36   C. 7 7/36   D. 7 12/36

8. Subtract: 5 4/7 − 3 3/4 8.____
   A. 1 23/28   B. 2 1/28   C. 2 1/3   D. 2 23/28

9. Multiply: 2 3/4 × 6 1/3 9.____
   A. 12 1/4   B. 13 1/4   C. 17 5/12   D. 18 5/12

10. Divide: 5 1/4 ÷ 1 1/2 10.____
    A. 3/7   B. 3 1/4   C. 3 1/2   D. 7 7/8

11. Add: 536.5 + .03 + 8.209 11.____
    A. .545009   B. .544739   C. 544.739   D. 545.009

12. Subtract: 879.3 − 57.64 12.____
    A. 3.029   B. 30.29   C. 821.66   D. 8216.6

13. Multiply: 4.87
             ×73.8

    A. 35.8406   B. 35.9406   C. 358.406   D. 359.406

14. Divide: 053√9.858
    A. 18.6   B. 18.7   C. 186   D. 187

15. Add: .5 + 1/4
    A. .075   B. .75   C. 5/4   D. 21/4

16. What is 4.4% of 48?
    A. 2.112   B. 10.90   C. 21.12   D. 211.2

17. 16 is what percent of 8?
    A. 1/2%   B. 5%   C. 50%   D. 200%

18. 24 is 48% of
    A. 2   B. 5   C. 50   D. 500

19. A set of stereo records sells for $26.00. It is discounted 12% for a special sale.
    What is the sale price?
    A. $3.12   B. $12.88   C. $14.00   D. $22.88

20.
TABLE A. ACME MORTGAGE COMPANY
$3200 LOAN – 3/4 OF 1% INTEREST

Month	Payment	Principal Paid/Month	Interest Paid/Month
1	$27.98	$25.58	$2.40
2	27.98	25.77	2.21
3	27.98	25.96	2.02
4	27.98	26.15	1.83
5	27.98	20.35	1.63
6	27.98	26.55	1.43
7	27.98	26.75	1.23
8	27.98	26.95	1.03
9	27.98	27.15	.83
10	27.98	27.35	.63
11	27.98	27.56	.42
12	27.93	27.77	.16
TOTAL	$335.82	$320.00	$15.82

Acme Mortgage Company charges 3/4 of 1% (.0075) on the unpaid balance per month. Bowman Mortgage Company charges 8% per year on the total loan.

3 (#1)

Which company charges the MOST amount of interest on a $320 loan held for one year?
- A. Bowman charges the most.
- B. Acme charges the most.
- C. Acme and Bowman charge the same.
- D. Insufficient information to determine.

21.
Percent of Auto Insurance Discounts for
High School Students with Certain
Grade Point Averages

Policy Coverage	Grade Point Average Percent of Discount		
	A	B	C
Liability	33 1/3%	33 1/3%	10%
Comprehensive	20%	10%	-
Collision	25%	20%	-

Waldo Brown has an A average. The regular 6-month amounts to be paid for insurance before discounts follow:

  Liability $18.00
  Comprehensive $20.00
  Collision $60.00
  Total $98.00

How much does Waldo pay for insurance for 6 months?
  A. $25.00   B. $48.00   C. $73.00   D. $146.00

22. Mrs. Ortiz had a fire in an apartment she owns. Repairing the damage will cost about $800. The apartment is valued at $11,000 and is insured for $10,000. Mrs. Ortiz had paid $28.00 a year for 12 years for her insurance. The insurance company will pay the full amount of the claim ($800).
Which of the following statements are TRUE?
I. The amount of the claim is more than the amount Mrs. Ortiz paid for the insurance.
II. The insurance company should pay $11,000 for this claim.
III. If the house had been completely burned, the insurance company would pay $11,000.
IV. The maximum claim Mrs. Ortiz could collect is $10,000.
The CORRECT answer is:
  A. I, IV   B. I, II   C. I, III   D. II, III

23. When two coins are tossed, what is the chance that both will be tails? 1 in ____.
  A. 1   B. 2   C. 3   D. 4

24. If 5 teams are in a football league, how many games are necessary to allow each team to play every team one time? _____ games.
   A. 10
   B. 15
   C. 20
   D. 25

25. Five women agreed to help collect money for the Salvation Army. They collected the following amounts: $43.00, $82.00, $16.00, $139.00, and $75.00. What was the AVERAGE amount collected?
   A. $70
   B. $71
   C. $75
   D. $355

26. From the following statements, determine the CORRECT conclusion.
   I. If Joe is a boxer, then Joe is strong.
   II. Joe is not strong.
   The CORRECT answer is:
   A. Joe is a boxer.
   B. Joe is not a boxer.
   C. Joe could be a boxer.
   D. All boxers are strong.

27. The graph shown at the right represents the distribution of the Rexroth family budget.
   How much would the Rexroths have to earn per month if they are to save $1,800 per year.
   A. $150
   B. $1,650
   C. $1,800
   D. $21,600

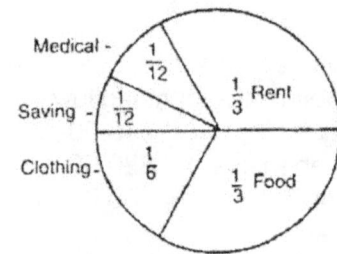

28.

	S	M	T	W	T	F	S
Mr. Tarver	?	8	8	8	8	8	3
Mr. Ramirez	1	8	9	9	8	8	5

Time and one-half is paid on Saturdays and for hours worked beyond 8 hours each day. Double-time is paid for Sunday work.
Mr. Tarver would have to work how many hours on Sunday to earn as much as Mr. Ramirez?
   Regular time: $2.00/hour
   Time and one-half: $3.00/hour
   Double time: $4.00/hour
   _____ hour(s).
   A. 1
   B. 4
   C. 5
   D. 16

29. Dorothy Cook wrote the following four checks:
   $93.47 for a portable radio
   $113.57 for groceries
   $7.95 for gasoline
   $12.65 for utilities

She deposited $42.96. The balance before the deposit and before the checks were written was $289.54.
After the checks were written and the deposit made, what was her new balance?
   A. $61.90   B. $104.86   C. $227.64   D. $270.60

30. Given the formula I = PRT:
If I = 27, R = .06, T = 3, find P.
   A. .0067   B. 1.5   C. 4.86   D. 150.00

30.____

31. Fencing is needed to enclose a piece of land 24 meters on a side.
How much fencing is needed?
_____ meters.
   A. 48
   B. 96
   C. 384
   D. 576

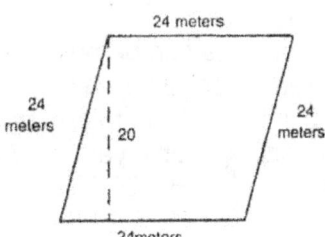

31.____

32. The area of figure A is 9 square units, and the area of B is 16 square units. What is the area of figure C?
_____ square units.
   A. 12
   B. 12 1/2
   C. 13
   D. 13 1/2

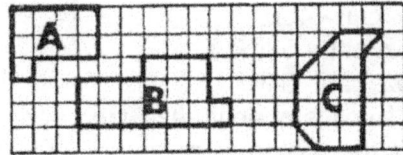

32.____

33. Using a 3 gallon spray can with a mixture rate of 1 teaspoon insecticide per quart of water and an application rate of 1 gallon of mixture per 100 square feet, how much water and how much insecticide will be needed to spray a 75 feet by 10 feet lawn?
_____ teaspoons of insecticide and _____ gallons of water.
   A. 30; 7 1/2   B. 30; 10   C. 15; 7 1/2   D. 20; 5

33.____

34. Frank Silva will carpet his living room which has the following dimensions. If Frank pays $6.00 per square yard for the carpet, how much will it cost to carpet the living room? (9 square feet – 1 square yard)
   A. $126
   B. $150
   C. $1,134
   D. $1,350

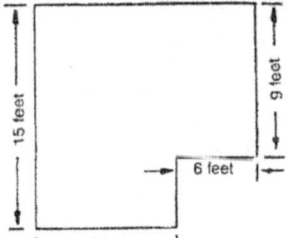

34.____

35. A cube is painted red and then divided into 27 smaller cubes.
How many of the smaller cubes are painted on three sides only?
   A. 6
   B. 8
   C. 10
   D. 12

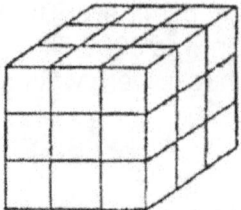

35.____

36. John and Frank wish to pour a cement walk 81 feet long, 4 feet wide, and 3 inches deep.
If ready-mix concrete can be delivered on weekdays for $19.50 a cubic yard and on weekends for $22.50 a cubic yard, how much would be saved on the complete job if they decide to purchase the cement on Wednesday rather than on the weekend? (1 cubic yard = 27 cubic feet)
   A. $3.00   B. $9.00   C. $27.00   D. $58.50

36.____

37. Antifreeze may be purchased in different size containers for different prices
   8 oz. can - 45¢
   10 oz. can - 53¢
   12 oz. can - 64¢
If exactly 15 pints of antifreeze are needed, how many cans of each size are needed for the cost to be minimum? (16 oz. = 1 pint)
   A. 10 – 12 oz. cans and 12 =10 oz. cans
   B. 20 – 12 oz. cans
   C. 24 – 10 oz. cans
   D. 15 – 12 oz. cans and 6 – 10 oz. cans

37.____

38. From the graph shown at the right, assuming the growth rate in the sophomore class is constant, how many students will be in the sophomore class in 2022?
   A. 325
   B. 350
   C. 375
   D. 400

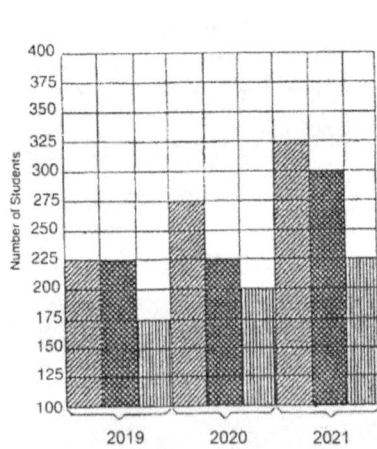

38.____

39.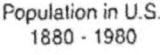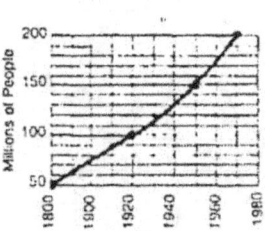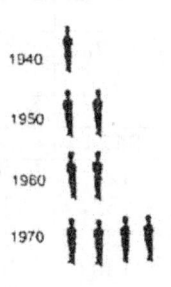

In looking at the two graphs, which of the following conclusions are TRUE?
I. Both graphs cover exactly the same period of time.
II. Both graphs show population growth.
III. In 1950 there were 150 million people in the U.S. and 3 million college students.
IV. In the general population of 200 million in 1970, 8 million students were in college.
V. The percentage of the college students remains the same in the period 1940 to 1970.
VI. In 1920 there were only 1 million college students out of 100 million people.
The CORRECT answer is:
  A. I, II, III   B. II, III, VI   C. II, V, VI   D. II, III, IV

40. Martin Owens owns a mountain cabin that has a market value of $9,000. Its assessed value is 25% of the market value. The tax rate is $11 per $100 of assessed value.
What is the amount of his tax?
  A. $24.75   B. $247.50   C. $495.00   D. $742.50

41. To finance a new state highway system decide to raise the gasoline tax. What information would be MOST helpful in establishing the amount of the raise?
  I. The total number of cars in the state
  II. The total number of gallons of gasoline sold in the last year
  III. The number of drivers under 21 years old
  IV. A table showing a rate of increase in gasoline sold from year to year
  V. A table showing the average number of miles driven per person
  VI. The number of small (4 cylinder) cars in the state
  VII. The number of car registrations sold each year
The CORRECT answer is:
  A. III, IV, VI   B. II, V, VII   C. I, V   D. II, IV

42.

INCOME TAX TABLE							
If adjusted gross income is		And the number of exemptions is					
		1	2	3	4	5	6
At least	But less than	Your tax is:					
$2,450	$2,475	$236	$124	$23	$0	0	$0
2,475	2,500	240	128	26	0	0	0
2,500	2,525	244	132	30	0	0	0
2,525	2,550	248	136	33	0	0	0
2,550	2,575	253	139	37	0	0	0
2,575	2,600	257	143	40	0	0	0
2,600	2,625	261	147	44	0	0	0
2,625	2,650	265	151	47	0	0	0
2,650	2,675	270	155	51	0	0	0
2,675	2,700	274	159	54	0	0	0
2,700	2,725	278	163	58	0	0	0
2,725	2,750	282	167	61	0	0	0
2,750	2,775	287	171	65	0	0	0
2,775	2,800	291	175	68	0	0	0
2,800	2,825	295	179	72	0	0	0
2,825	2,850	299	183	76	0	0	0
2,850	2,875	304	187	79	0	0	0

Alvie Ramos earned $2,856.00 during his senior year in high school.
To find his adjusted gross income, he must reduce the amount earned by the standard 10% deduction. He had only one exemption, himself.
How much tax did Alvie pay?
   A. $139   B. $187   C. $253   D. $304

43.

Weight in Ounces	4 oz.	6 oz.	9 oz.	12 oz.	15 oz.
Price	2¢	4¢	7¢	10¢	13¢

Using the above table, predict the price if the weight in ounces is 25.
   A. 23¢   B. 24¢   C. 26¢   D. 27¢

44. Given [(0,3),(1,5),(2,7),...(5,y)]
What is the value for y?
   A. 9   B. 11   C. 13   D. 15

45. What is 4% of $14,000?
   A. $560   B. $35   C. $56   D. $350

KEY (CORRECT ANSWERS)

1.	B	11.	C	21.	C	31.	B	41.	B
2.	A	12.	C	22.	A	32.	C	42.	C
3.	D	13.	D	23.	D	33.	A	43.	A
4.	B	14.	C	24.	A	34.	A	44.	C
5.	C	15.	B	25.	B	35.	B	45.	A
6.		16.	A	26.	B	36.	B		
7.	C	17.	D	27.	C	37.	C		
8.	A	18.	C	28.	B	38.	C		
9.	C	19.	D	29.	B	39.	D		
10.	C	20.	A	30.	D	40.	B		

10 (#1)

SOLUTIONS TO PROBLEMS

1. $4898 + 7 + 361 + 26 = 5292$

2. $7006 - 5797 = 1209$

3. $(2579)(806) = 2{,}223{,}754$

4. $72{,}732 \div 87 = 836$

5. $(-6) - (-4) \_ (-3) = 6 + 4 - 3 = +7$

6. $[(-7)(-8) \div (-4) = \frac{56}{-4} = -14$

7. $1\ 4/9 + 5\ 3/4 = 1\ 16/36 + 5\ 27/36 = 6\ 43/36 = 7\ 7/36$

8. $5\ 4/7 - 3\ 3/4 = 5\ 16/28 - 3\ 21/28 = 4\ 44/28 - 3\ 31/28 = 1\ 23/28$

9. $(2\ 3/4)(6\ 1/3) = (11/4P)(19/3) = 209/12 = 16\ 5/12$

10. $5\ 1/4 \div 1\ 1/2 = (21/8)(2/3) = 42/12 = 3\ 1/2$

11. $536.5 + .03 + 8.209 = 544.739$

12. $879.3 - 57.64 = 821.66$

13. $(4.87)(73.8) == 359.406$

14. $9.858 \div .053 = 186$

15. $.5 + 1/4 = .5 + .25 = .75$

16. $(4.4\%)(48) = (.044)(48) = 2.112$

17. $16/8 = 2 = 200\%$

18. $24 \div 48 = 50$

19. $\$26 - (\$26)(.12) = \$22.88$

20. Acme charges $15.82 in interest, whereas Bowman charges $(\$320)(.08) = \$25.60$ in interest. Thus, Bowman charges the most.

21. Total payment = $(\$18)(66\ 2/3\%) + (\$20)(80\%) + (\$60)(75\%) = \$73.00$

22. Statements I, IV are correct. Note that she paid $(\$28)(12) = \$336$ in insurance vs. the amount of the claim ($800). Also, since her house was insured for $10,000, that is the maximum amount she could receive for a claim.

11 (#1)

23. Probability of 2 tails = 1/2 . 1/2 = 1/4 = 1 in 4

24. (5)(4) ÷ 2 = 10 games. This is actually the number of combinations of 5 items taken 2 at a time.

25. ($43 + $82 + $16 + $139 + 75) ÷ 5 = $71

26. The conclusion is *Joe is not a boxer*. Let p = Joe is a boxer, q = Joe is strong. The contrapositive of *If p then q* is *If not q then not p*.

27. Earnings = (12)(savings), so that (12)($1800) = $21,600 earnings per year = $21,600 ÷ 12 = $1800 earnings per month.

28. Mr. Ramirez' earnings = (40)($2) + (7)($3) + (1)($4) = $105. So far, Mr. Tarver has earned ($40)(2) + ($3)(3) = $89

29. New balance = $289.54 + $42.96 - $93.47 - $113.57 - $7.95 - $12.65 = $104.86

30. 27 = (P)(.06)(3), so P = 27 ÷ 18 = 150

31. Fencing needed = (24)(4) = 96 meters

32. Area of C = (4)(5) − (1/2)(2)(2) − (1/2)(1)(1) − 4 1/2 = 13 sq. units

33. (75)(10) ÷ 100 = 7.5 gallons of spray. Since 7.5 gallons = 30 quarts, 30 teaspoons of insecticide and 7 1/2 gallons of water are needed.

34. Area = (15)(15) − (6)(6) = 189 sq.ft. = 21 sq.yds.
    Then, the cost = (21)($6) = $126

35. The cubes which are painted on 3 sides will be the 8 cubes in the corners.

36. Savings = [(27)(1 1/3)(1/12)][$22.50 - $19.50] = $9.00

37. For A: Cost = (10)(.64) + (12)(.53) = $12.76
    For B: Cost = (20)(.64) = $12.80
    For C: Cost = (24)(.53) = $12.72
    For D: Cost = (15)(.64) + (6)(.53) = $12.78
    Option C has the minimum cost.

38. Growth rate = 50 per year. Number of sophomores in 2022 = 325 + 50 = 375

39. Statements II, III, IV are correct. Statement I is wrong since one graph covers 1880-1980, whereas the other graph covers 1940-1970. Statement V is wrong since the percentage of college students increases from 1940 to 1970. Statement VI is unverifiable since the second chart does not include 1920.

40. Assessed value = (.25)($9000) = $2250. The tax = ($11)($2250/$100) = $247.50

12 (#1)

41. The only statements pertinent to gasoline taxes would be II, V, and VII.

42. ($2856)(.90) = $2570.40. This number is found between $2550 and $2575 on the chart. Using the column for 1 exemption, the tax = $253.

43. The price in cents is 2 numbers below the number of ounces. Given 25 ounces, the price = 23 cents.

44. (5,y) corresponds to the sixth point. In the sequence 3, 5, 7,..., the sixth number is 13.

45. (.04)($14,000) = $560

EXAMINATION SECTION
TEST 1

DIRECTIONS: Each question or incomplete statement is followed by several suggested answers or completions. Select the one that BEST answers the question or completes the statement. *PRINT THE LETTER OF THE CORRECT ANSWER IN THE SPACE AT THE RIGHT.*

1. Which of the following fractions is the SMALLEST?   1.____
 A. 2/3   B. 4/5   C. 5/7   D. 5/11

2. 40% is equivalent to which of the following?   2.____
 A. 4/5   B. 4/6   C. 2/5   D. 4/100

3. How many 100's are in 10,000?   3.____
 A. 10   B. 100   C. 10,000   D. 100,000

4. $\frac{6}{7} + \frac{11}{12}$ is approximately   4.____
 A. 1   B. 2   C. 17   D. 19

5. The time required to heat water to a certain temperature is directly proportional to the volume of water being heated.
 If it takes 12 minutes to heat 1 ½ gallons of water, how many minutes will it take to heat 2 gallons of water?   5.____
 A. 12   B. 16   C. 18   D. 24

6. The cost of an item increased by 25%.
 If the original cost was C dollars, identify the expression which gives the new cost of that item.   6.____
 A. C + 0.25   B. 1/4 C   C. 25C   D. 1.25C

7. Given the formula PV = nRT, all of the following are true EXCEPT   7.____
 A. T = PV/nR   B. P = nRTN   C. V = P/nRT   D. n = PV/RT

8. If a Fahrenheit (F) temperature reading is 104, find its Celsius (C) equivalent, given that C = i(F-32).   8.____
 A. 36   B. 40   C. 72   D. 76

9. If 40% of a graduating class plans to go directly to work after graduation, which of the following must be TRUE?   9.____
 A. Less than half of the class plans to go directly to work.
 B. Forty members of the class plan to enter the job market.
 C. Most of the class plans to go directly to work.
 D. Six in ten members of the class are expected not to graduate.

10. Given a multiple-choice test item which has 5 choices, what is the probability of guessing the correct answer if you know nothing about the item content?
    A. 5%   B. 10%   C. 20%   D. 25%

11.

S	T
0	80
5	75
10	65
15	50
20	30
25	5

Which graph BEST represents the data shown in the above table?

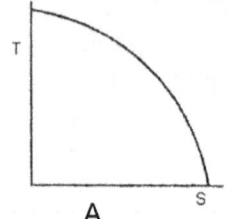
A

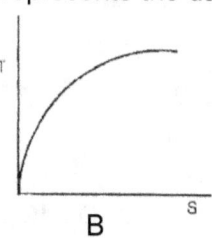
B

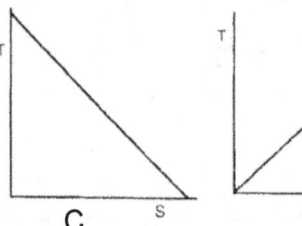
C   D

12. If 3(x+5y) = 24, find y when x = 3.
    A. 1   B. 3   C. 33/5   D. 7

13. The payroll of a grocery store for its 23 clerks is $395,421.
    Which expression below shows the average salary of a clerk?
    A. 395,421 × 23   B. 23 ÷ 395,421
    C. (395,421 × 23   D. 395,421 ÷ 23

14. If 12.8 pounds of coffee cost $50.80, what is the APPROXIMATE price per pound?
    A. $2.00   B. $3.00   C. $4.00   D. $5.00

15. A road map has a scale where 1 inch corresponds to 150 miles.
    A distance of 3 3/4 inches on the map corresponds to what actual distance?
    _____ miles.
    A. 153.75   B. 375   C. 525   D. 562.5

16. How many square feet of plywood are needed to construct the back and 4 adjacent sides of the box shown at the right?
    A. 63
    B. 90
    C. 96
    D. 126

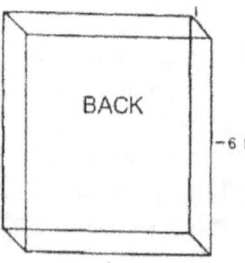

17. One thirty-pound bag of lawn fertilizer costs $20.00 and will cover 600 square feet of lawn. Terry's lawn is a 96 foot by 75 foot rectangle. How much will it cost Terry to buy enough bags of fertilizer for her lawn?
    Which of the following do you NOT need in order to solve this problem? The
    A. product of 96 and 75
    B. fact that one bag weighs 30 pounds
    C. fact that one bag covers 600 square feet
    D. fact that one bag costs $20.00

17.____

18. On the graph shown at the right, between which hours was the drop in temperature GREATEST?
    A. 11:00 – Noon
    B. Noon – 1:00
    C. 1:00 – 2:00
    D. 2:00 – 3:00

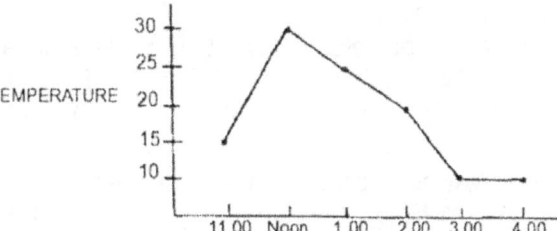

18.____

19. If on a typical railroad track the distance from the center of one railroad tie to the next is 30 inches, approximately how many ties would be needed for one mile of track?
    A. 180   B. 2,110   C. 6,340   D. 63,360

19.____

20. Which of the following is MOST likely to be the volume of a wine bottle?
    A. 750 milliliters   B. 7 kilograms
    C. 7 milligrams   D. 7 liters

20.____

21. What is the reading on the gauge shown at the right?
    A. -7
    B. -3
    C. 1
    D. 3

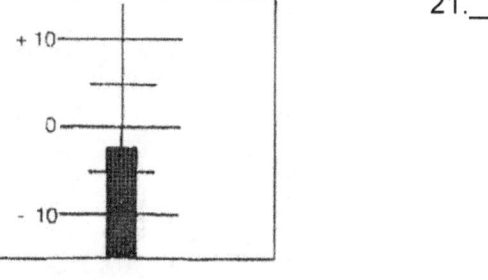

21.____

22. Which statement below disproves the assertion, *All students in Mrs. Marino's 10th grade geometry class are planning to go to college?*
    A. Albert is in Mrs. Marino's class, but he is not planning to take mathematics next year.
    B. Jorge is not in Mrs. Marino's class, but he is still planning to go to college.
    C. Pierre is in Mrs. Marino's class but says he will not be attending school anymore after this year.
    D. Crystal is in Mrs. Marino's class and plans to attend Yale University when she graduates.

22.____

23. A store advertisement reads, *Buy not while our prices are low. There will never be a better time to buy.*
    The customer reading this advertisement should assume that
    A. the prices at the store will probably never be lower
    B. right now, this store has the best prices in town
    C. prices are higher at other stores
    D. prices are always lowest at this store

24. *Given any positive integer, there is always a positive number B such that A × B is less than 1.*
    Which statement below supports this generalization?
    A. 8 × 1/16 = 1/2
    B. 8 × 1/2 = 4
    C. 5/2 × 1/10 = 1/4
    D. 1/2 × 1/2 = 1/2

25. Of the following expressions, which is equivalent to 4C + D = 12E?
    A. C = 4(12E-D)
    B. 4 + D = 12E − C
    C. 4C + 12E = -D
    D. $C = \frac{12E-D}{4}$

KEY (CORRECT ANSWERS)

1.	D		11.	A
2.	C		12.	A
3.	B		13.	D
4.	B		14.	C
5.	B		15.	D
6.	D		16.	C
7.	C		17.	B
8.	B		18.	D
9.	A		19.	B
10.	C		20.	A

21.	B
22.	C
23.	A
24.	A
25.	D

SOLUTIONS TO PROBLEMS

1. Converting to decimals, we get $.\overline{6}$, .8, .714 (approx..), $.\overline{45}$. The smallest is $.\overline{45}$ corresponding to 5/11.

2. 40% = 40/100 = 2/5

3. 10,000 ÷ 100 = 100

4. $\frac{6}{7} + \frac{11}{12}$ = (72+77) ÷ 84 = $\frac{149}{84}$ ≈ 1.77 ≈ 2

5. Let x = required minutes. Then, 12/1 ½ = x^2. This reduces to 1 1/2x = 24. Solving, x = 16.

6. New cost is C + .25C = 1.25C

7. For PV = nRT, V = nRT/P

8. C = 5/9 (104-32) = 5/9(72) = 40

9. Since 40% is less than 50% (or half), we conclude that less than half of the class plans to go to work directly after graduation.

10. The probability of guessing right is 1/5 or 20%

11. Curve A is most accurate since as S increases, we see that T decreases. Note, however, that the relationship is NOT linear. Although S increases in equal amounts, the decrease in T is NOT in equal amounts.

12. 3(3+5y) = 24. This simplifies to 9 + 15y = 24. Solving, y = 1

13. The average salary is $395,421 ÷ 23

14. The price per pound is $50.80 ÷ 12.8 = $3,96875 or approximately $4.

15. Actual distance is (3 3/4)(150) = 562.5 miles.

16. The area of the back = (6)(5) = 30 sq. ft. The combined area of the two vertical sides is (2)(6)(3) = 36 sq. ft. The combined area of the horizontal sides is (2)(5)(3) = 30 sq. ft. Total area = 30 + 36 30 = 96 square feet.

17. Choice B is not relevant to solving the problem since the cost will be [(96)(75)/600][$20] = $240. So, the weight per bag is not needed.

18. For the graph, the largest temperature drop was from 2:00 P.M. to 3:00 P.M. The temperature dropped 20 – 10 = 10 degrees.

6 (#1)

19. 1 mile = 5280 feet = 63,360 inches. Then, 63,360 ÷ 30 = 2112 or about 2110 ties are needed.

20. Since 1 liter = 1.06 quarts, 750 milliliters = (750/1000)(1.06) = .795 quarts. This is a reasonable volume for a wine bottle.

21. The reading is -3.

22. Statement C contradicts the given information, since Pierre is in Mrs. Marino's class. Then he should plan to go to college.

23. Since there will never be a better time to buy at this particular store, the customer can assume the current prices will probably never be lower.

24. Statement A illustrates this concept. Note that in general, if n is a positive integer. then $(n)(\frac{1}{n-1}) < 1$

25. _____

TEST 2

DIRECTIONS: Each question or incomplete statement is followed by several suggested answers or completions. Select the one that BEST answers the question or completes the statement. *PRINT THE LETTER OF THE CORRECT ANSWER IN THE SPACE AT THE RIGHT.*

1. Which of the following lists numbers in INCREASING order?
   A. 0.4, 0.04, 0.004
   B. 2.71, 3.15, 2.996
   C. 0.7, 0.77, 0.777
   D. 0.06, 0.5, 0.073

2. $\frac{4}{10}+\frac{7}{100}+\frac{5}{1000} =$
   A. 4.75
   B. 0.475
   C. 0.0475
   D. 0.00475

3. 700 times what number equals 7?
   A. 10
   B. 0.1
   C. 0.01
   D. 0.001

4. 943-251 is approximately
   A. 600
   B. 650
   C. 700
   D. 1200

5. The time needed to set up a complicated piece of machinery is inversely proportional to the number of years' experience of the worker.
   If a worker with 10 years' experience needs 6 hours to do the job, how long will it take a worker with 15 years' experience?
   A. 4
   B. 5
   C. 9
   D. 25

6. Let W represent the number of waiters and D, the number of diners in a particular restaurant.
   Identify the expression which represents the statement: There are 10 times as many diners as waiters.
   A. 10W = D
   B. 10D = W
   C. 10D + 10W
   D. 10 = D + W

7. Which of the following is equivalent to the formula F = XC + Y?
   A. F − C = X + Y
   B. Y = F + XC
   C. $C = \frac{FY}{X}$
   D. $C = \frac{FX}{Y}$

8. Given the formula A = BC/D, if A = 12, B = 6, and D = 3, what is the value of C?
   A. 2/3
   B. 6
   C. 18
   D. 24

9. 5 is to 7 as X is to 35. X =
   A. 7
   B. 12
   C. 24
   D. 49

10. Kramer Middle School has 5 seventh grade mathematics teachers: two of the math teachers are women and three are men.
    If you are assigned a teacher at random, what is the probability of getting a female teacher?
    A. 0.2
    B. 0.4
    C. 0.6
    D. 0.8

11. Which statement BEST describes the graph shown at the right?
    Temperature
    A. and time decrease at the same rate
    B. and time increase at the same rate
    C. increases over time
    D. decreases over time

12. If $3x + 4 = 22y$, find y when $x = 2$.
    A. 0   B. 3   C. 4 1/2   D. 5

13. A car goes 243 miles on 8.7 gallons of gas.
    Which numeric expression should be used to determine the car's miles per gallon?
    A. 243 × 87   B. 8.7 ÷ 243   C. 243 ÷ 8.7   D. 243 − 8.7

14. What is the average cost per book if you buy six books at $4.00 each and four books at $5.00 each?
    A. $4.40   B. $4.50   C. $4.60   D. $5.40

15. A publisher's sale offers a 15% discount to anyone buying more than 100 workbooks.
    What will be the discount on 200 workbooks selling at $2.25 each?
    A. $15.00   B. $30.00   C. $33.75   D. $67.50

16. A road crew erects 125 meters of fencing in one workday.
    How many workdays are required to erect a kilometer of fencing?
    A. 0.8   B. 8   C. 80   D. 800

17. Last month Kim made several telephone calls to New York City totaling 45 minutes in all.
    What does Kim need in order to calculate the average duration of her New York City calls?
    The
    A. total number of calls she made to New York City
    B. cost per minute of a call to New York City
    C. total cost of her telephone bill last month
    D. days of the week on which the calls are made

18.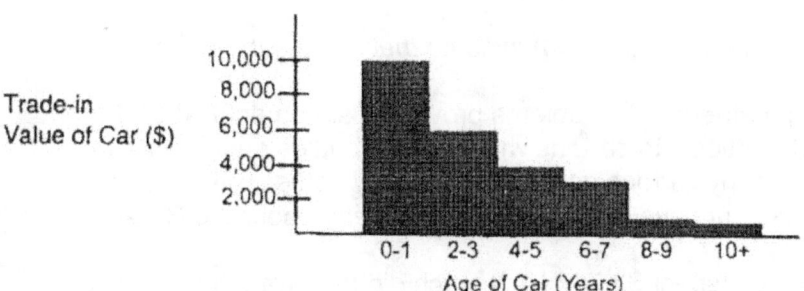

The above chart relates a car's age to its trade-in value.
Based on the chart, which of the following is TRUE?
A. A 4- to 5-year old car has a trade-in value of about $2,000
B. The trade-in vale of an 8- to 9-year old car is about 1/3 that of a 2- to 3-year old car.
C. A 6- to 7-year old car has no trade-in value.
D. A 4- to 5-year old car's trade-in value is about $2,000 less than that of a 2- to 3-year old car.

19. Which of the following expressions could be used to determine how many seconds are in a 24-hour day?
A. 60 × 60 × 24
B. 60 × 12 × 24
C. 60 × 2 × 24
D. 60 × 24

20. For measuring milk, we could use each of the following EXCEPT
A. liters
B. kilograms
C. millimeters
D. cubic centimeters

21. What is the reading on the gauge shown at the right?
A. 51
B. 60
C. 62.5
D. 70

22. Bill is taller than Yvonne. Yvonne is shorter than Sue. Sue is 5' tall.
Which of the following conclusions must be TRUE?
A. Bill is taller than Sue.
B. Yvonne is taller than 5'4".
C. Sue is taller than Bill.
D. Yvonne is the shortest.

23. The Bass family traveled 268 miles during the first day of their vacation and another 300 miles on the next day. Maria Bass said they were 568 miles from home.
Which of the following facts did Maria assume?
A. They traveled faster on the first day and slower on the second.
B. If she plotted the vacation route on a map, it would be a straight line.
C. Their car used more gasoline on the second day.
D. They traveled faster on the second day than they did on the first day.

24. *The word LEFT in a mathematics problem indicate that it is a subtraction problem.*
    Which of the following mathematics problems prove this statement FALSE?
    A. I want to put 150 bottles into cartons which hold 8 bottles each. After I completely fill as many cartons as I can, how many bottles will be left?
    B. Sarah has 5 books but gave one to John. How many books did Sarah have left?
    C. Carlos had $4.25 but spent $3.75. How much did he have left?
    D. We had 38 models in stock but after yesterday's sale, only 12 are left. How many did we sell?

25. Let Q represent the number of miles Dave can jog in 15 minutes.
    Identify the expression which represents the number of miles Dave can jog between 3:00 P.M. and 4:45 P.M.
    A. 1 3/4 Q   B. 7Q   C. 15 × 1 3/4 × Q   D. Q/7

KEY (CORRECT ANSWERS)

1.	C		11.	D
2.	B		12.	D
3.	C		13.	C
4.	C		14.	A
5.	A		15.	D
6.	A		16.	B
7.	C		17.	A
8.	B		18.	D
9.	C		19.	A
10.	B		20.	C

21. C
22. D
23. B
24. A
25. B

SOLUTIONS TO PROBLEMS

1. Choice C is in ascending order since $.y < .77 < .777$

2. Rewrite in decimal form: $.4 + .07 + .005 = .475$

3. Let x = missing number. Then, $700x = 7$. Solving, $x = 7/700 = .01$

4. $943 - 251 = 692 \approx 700$

5. Let x = hours needed. Then, $10/15 = x/6$. Solving, $x = 4$

6. The number of diners (D) is 10 times as many waiters (10W). So, $D = 10W$, or $10W = D$

7. Given $F = XC + Y$, subtract Y from each side to get $F - Y = XC$. Finally, dividing by X, we get $(F-Y)/X = C$

8. $12 = 6C/3$. Then, $12 = 2C$, so $C = 6$

9. $5/7 = x/35$. Then, $7x = 175$, so $x = 25$

10. Probability of a female teacher = $2/5 = .4$

11. Statement D is best, since as time increases, the temperature decreases.

12. $(3)(2) + 4 = 2y$. Then, $10 = 2y$, so $y = 5$.

13. Miles per gallon = $243/8.7$

14. Total purchase is $(6)(\$4) + (4)(\$5) = \$44$. The average cost per book is $\$44 \div 10 = \$4.40$

15. $(220)(\$2.25) = \$450$. The discount is $(.15)(\$450) = \$67.50$

16. The number of workdays is $1000 \div 125 = 8$

17. Choice A is correct because the average duration of the phone calls = total time ÷ total number of calls.

18. Statement D is correct since a 4-5 year old car's value is $4,000, whereas a 2-3 year-old car's value is $6000.

19. 60 seconds = 1 minute and 60 minutes = 1 hour. Thus, 24 hours = $(24)(60)(60)$ or $(60)(60)(24)$ seconds.

20. We can't use millimeters in measuring milk since millimeters is a linear measurement.

21. The reading shows the average of 50 and $75 = 62.5$

6 (#2)

22. Since Yvonne is shorter than both Bill and Sue, Yvonne is the shortest.

23. Statement B is assumed correct since 568 = 269 + 300 could only be true if the mileage traveled represents a straight line.

24. To find the number of bottles left, we look only for the remainder when 150 is divided b 8 (which happens to be 6).

25. 3:00 P.M. to 4:45 P.M. = 1 hour and 45 minutes = 105 minutes
Let Q = 15 minutes
105 / 15 = 7
7(15) = 105 = 7Q

BASIC PRINCIPLES AND PRACTICES IN EDUCATION
THE NEW PROGRAM OF EDUCATION

CONTENTS

	Page
I. PHILOSOPHY AND OBJECTIVES	1
A. Philosophy	1
B. Concepts of Education	1
C. Objectives	1
D. Methods of Achieving These Objectives	2
E. Organismic Psychology	2
F. Underlying Tenets of the Program	2
G. What Does the New Program Mean?	3
H. Advantages and Disadvantages	3
I. Traditional vs. Progressive Education General Principles	4
J. in Any Modern Philosophy of Elementary Education	5
II. THE CURRICULUM	5
A. Definitions	5
B. General Considerations	5
C. Conditions that Compel Curricular Changes	6
D. Changes that Result From Curriculum Improvement	6
E. Main Problems in Curriculum Development	7
F. Factors Affecting Curriculum Programs	7
G. Considerations for Curriculum Programs	7
H. Questions Related to Curriculum Development	7
III. GROUPING AND COMMITTEE WORK	8
A. Organizing Groups for Instruction	8
B. Criteria for Group Work	8
C. Committee Work	9
IV. EVALUATION	10
A. Items to be Evaluated	10
B. Reasons for Evaluating	10
C. Who Evaluates?	10
D. Evaluation in a Unit of Work	10
V. DISCIPLINE	12
A. Meaning	12
B. Discipline vs. Order	12
C. The Difference Between Conduct and Behavior	12

	Page
V. DISCIPLINE (cont'd)	12
D. Planes of Discipline	12
E. General Principles of Classroom Discipline	13
F. Positive vs. Negative Discipline	13
G. Why Some Teachers Have Disciplinary Troubles	13
H. Class Morale as a Factor in Classroom Discipline	13
I. The Use of Incentives	14
J. Classroom Punishments	16
K. Some Practical Suggestions for Teachers (Characteristic of Transition from Order to Discipline)	17
VI. BASIC FUNDAMENTALS OF EDUCATIONAL PSYCHOLOGY	17
A. Conditioning	17
B. Learning by Trial and Error (Connectionism)	18
C. Learning by Insight: Gestalt Psychology	18
D. The Field Theory (Organismic, Holistic Theory)	19
E. Transfer of Training	19
F. Habit	20
G. Individual Differences	21
VII. HISTORY OF EDUCATION	22
A. Leaders	22
1. Socrates	22
2. Plato	22
3. Aristotle	22
4. Comenius	23
5. Locke	23
6. Rousseau	23
7. Basedow	23
8. Pestalozzi	23
9. Herbart	24
10. Froebel	24
11. Spencer	24
12. Mann	24
13. Barnard	24
14. Dewey	24
B. Conceptualized Definitions and Aims of Education	24

BASIC PRINCIPLES AND PRACTICES IN EDUCATION
THE NEW PROGRAM OF EDUCATION

I. PHILOSOPHY AND OBJECTIVES

A. PHILOSOPHY
1. An analysis of the aims and purposes of education
2. An appraisal of current educational practices
3. A statement of the "ideal" to be attained
4. A justification of the means to be employed

B. CONCEPTS OF EDUCATION
1. Education as knowledge
   a. Emphasis on factual learning
   b. Transmitting the past heritage
   c. Excessive use of texts
2. Education as discipline
   a. Training the memory, imagination, etc.
   b. Emphasis on rote memory, drill, frequent tests, etc.
   c. Reliance on theory of transfer of training
3. Education as growth
   a. Developing latent capacities and realization of child's potentialities
   b. Experiential and functional learning
   c. Emphasis on attitudes, appreciations, and interests
   d. Child-centered curriculum
   e. Stress on social relationships and democratic living procedures

C. OBJECTIVES
1. Character - ethical living in a society promoting the common welfare
2. American Heritage - faith in American democracy and respect for dignity and worth of the individual regardless of race, religion, nationality or socio-economic status
3. Health - sound body and wholesome mental and emotional development
4. Exploration - discovery and development of individual aptitudes
5. Thinking - develop ability to reason critically, using facts and principles
6. Knowledges and skills - command of common integrating knowledges and skills
7. Appreciation and expression - appreciation and enjoyment of beauty and development of powers of creative expression
8. Social relationships - develop desirable social relationships at home, in school, in the community
9. Economic relationships - appreciation of economic processes and of contributions of all who serve in the world of work

MNEMONIC DEVICE FOR REMEMBERING THESE OBJECTIVES

T hinking   K nowledges and skills
E xploration   A ppreciation
A merican heritage   S ocial relationships
C haracter   E conomic relationships
H ealth

D. METHOD OF ACHIEVING THESE OBJECTIVES
1. Former emphasis on content with limited worthwhile, real experiences. Present stress on experiences with content used as a means to an end rather than as an end in itself.
2. This calls for a reorganization of our courses of study. Organization will now be in related areas rather than in separate isolated syllabi. These areas include:
    a. Pupil participation - to include planning, routines, and housekeeping, responsibilities, exploring school and community activities.
    b. Health - to include health instruction and guidance, safety education, rest, recreation, emotional adjustment, nutrition.
    c. Art - to include experimenting, use of various media as means of expression, practical applications in home, school, and community.
    d. Music - vocal, instrumental, rhythmic for enjoyment, expression, and understanding.
    e. Language Arts - reading, literature, composition, spelling, penmanship, speech, listening, dramatization.
    f. Social Studies - history, geography, civics, character, family relationships, consumer problems, intercultural education, citizenship and concepts of democracy.
    g. Science - nature study, weather, plants and soil, animals, earth and sky, food and water, tools and instruments, simple machines and electrical devices, flightcraft.
    h. Arithmetic - size, space, distance, time, weight, concepts, computations, problem solving.

MNEMONIC DEVICE FOR THESE AREAS

H ealth	L anguage Arts
A rithmetic	A rt
S ocial Studies	M usic
	P upil participation
	S cience

E. ORGANISMIC PSYCHOLOGY *(our current program is based chiefly on these principles)*
1. The principle of continuous growth - This emphasizes the flexible, experimental, emergent nature of the individual and of society; it stresses the continuity of experience. (Aspects: continuous progress plan; constant curriculum revision.)
2. The principle of experience as the method of learning - This emphasizes learning through functional, real experiences as opposed to memorization, drill, dictated assignments, etc. (Aspects: excursions; planning; research; reporting.)
3. The principal of integration - This emphasizes the wholeness and unity of individuals and of society. It stresses the interaction between the learner and the learning situation and demands maximum life-likeness in learning situations. (Aspects: units; use of community resources; large areas of instruction; larger time-blocks.)

F. UNDERLYING TENETS OF THE PROGRAM
1. Education of the whole child - social, civic, intellectual, ethical, vocational
2. Learning through real, functional experiences (activity vs. passivity)

3. The "intangibles" as an important end of education (interests, attitudes, character, etc.)
4. The concept of the child-centered school as opposed to the subject-centered school
5. The inclusion of the nine objectives of education as a part of educational planning at every step

G. WHAT DOES THE NEW PROGRAM MEAN?
1. These things are basic:
    a. Socialization of procedures
    b. Integration of personality (before integration of subject matter)
    c. Increased pupil-teacher participation in planning and evaluating the educative process
    d. Group procedures
    e. A program to meet the individual's time-table of grewth as well as a general development time-table
    f. First-hand experiencing as a "must" in education
    g. A mental hygiene viewpoint for the teacher
    h. Closer relationship between school-life and life in the world outside
    i. An acceptance of the view that concomitant learnings can sometimes be more important than the original learnings to be taught
2. It is NOT merely:
    a. Unit development
    b. Correlation of subject matter
    c. Working through committees
    d. Provision for research activities
    e. Emphasis on reporting and discussion
    f. Planning for a culmination
    g. Keeping diaries and logs

H. ADVANTAGES AND DISADVANTAGES
1. Proponents of the New Program maintain that this program:
    a. Provides a flexible content
    b. Encourages individual aptitudes
    c. Permits much practice in social behavior
    d. Encourages independent learning
    e. Encourages creative expression
    f. Provides a vitalized curriculum
    g. Permits greater integration of subject matter
    h. Provides for leisure-time activities
    i. Provides a success program for each child
    j. Makes greater provision for diagnosis, guidance, and individual remedial treatment
    k. Contributes abundantly towards the development of good character
2. Opponents of the New Program maintain that:
    a. There is no gradation of the difficulties of different units of work
    b. It is not true to life (since life is not a series of activities)
    c. Too much reliance is placed on incidental learning
    d. There is no provision for participation by every child
    e. Teachers have not been trained sufficiently
    f. Equipment is underemphasized

g. The interests of children are not sufficient as a guide for subject matter
h. The superficial aspects are overemphasized
i. Many important "learnings" are omitted
j. No provision is made for duplication in the case of pupils who are transferred or admitted

I. TRADITIONAL VS. PROGRESSIVE EDUCATION

TRADITIONAL	PROGRESSIVE
1. PHILOSOPHY	
a. School is a preparation for life	a. School is "life itself" life
b. Emphasis on social heritage	b. Development of whole personality-knowledge, attitudes, morals, health
c. Adjust pipil to society that arises	c. School aims to improve society
2. CURRICULUM	
a. Factual curriculum laid out in advance for all	a. Subject matter -vital, purposeful, integrated, flexible, follows child's interests
b. Subjects clearly separated and isolated	b. Long units, integration and correlation of subject matter
c. Emphasis on memorization	c. Learning through experiences
d. Slavish use of text books	d. Use of a variety of reference and source materials
3. ROLE OF TEACHER	
a. Dominant factor in the learning process	a. Teacher is a guide and helper
b. Pupil passivity	b. Socialization and maximum pupil participation
4. METHODS	
a. Stressed mastery of subject	a. Adjustment of curriculum to matter needs, interests, and capacities of each child
b. Isolated drills. Extrinsic	b. Functional learning. Individualized drill at the point of error. Intrinsic
c. Rigid, formal discipline	c. A hum of activity. Self-discipline. Social adjustment
d. Inside of schoolroom	d. Excursions and field trips
5. SUPERVISION	
a. Dictatorial and inflexible	a. Democratic, scientific, creative
b. Teachers rated according to ability in achieving grade standards (standardized ap-tests)	b. Teachers judged on basis of their ability to promote desirable attitudes - interests, preciations, etc. (attitude tests and case histories)

J. GENERAL PRINCIPLES IN ANY MODERN PHILOSOPHY OF ELEMENTARY EDUCATION
   1. Education must be democratic, universal, and compulsory
   2. There must be a unifying philosophy for the school system as a whole
   3. This philosophy must be essentially a social philosophy; the school must adjust children to a changing social order
   4. The curriculum must be flexible and must be subject to frequent (continuous) revision
   5. There must be flexibility in classroom procedures
   6. Adequate equipment must be provided
   7. Adequate provision must be made for the mentally and physically handicapped

II. THE CURRICULUM

A. DEFINITIONS
   1. The CURRICULUM consists of all the experiences, including all the subject matter and skills, which are utilized and interpreted by the school to further the aims of education. These experiences result from interaction between persons, influences, and material facilities. Some of the factors which effect the curriculum are:
      a. The political, economic, and social structure of the surrounding society
      b. The public opinion toward education
      c. The aims and philosophies of those operating the educational system
      d. The decisions concerning methods and materials, teacher selection, sarlaries, and physical plant
      e. The course of study, or, more properly, the documents made available to the teachers
   2. Early COURSES OF STUDY usually consisted only of a subject-matter outline; later ones included also some suggested learning activities, teaching procedures, diagnostic devices, and evaluation techniques. The emphasis, in all instances, was on "prescribed" subject matter to be covered, and some courses of study even specified the number of minutes per day to be devoted to each of the segments and the specific fact questions to be used.
   3. Modern GUIDES for teachers are not usually called courses of study. They suggest a wealth of materials and experiences; far from minimizing subject matter, they suggest more of it better adapted for use with varying levels of abilities and interests. They include bulletins on:
      a. the teaching of various subjects
      b. the organization of experience units with subject lines disregarded
      c. the characteristics of children
      d. varied learning experiences
      e. teaching procedures
      f. ways of using different types and amounts of subject matter
      g. sources of instructional aids
      h. evaluational techniques
      i. bibliographies, etc.

B. GENERAL CONSIDERATIONS
   1. A curriculum develops in answer to the needs of a group of learners and to the demands of a given society.

2. A curriculum is made by a teacher and her pupils as they work together in the school.
3. The development of a specific curriculum is a cooperative activity in which many persons participate (superintendents, principals, teachers, subject-matter specialists, consultants, school psychologists, pupils, parents, social agencies, advisory commissions, etc.)
4. A program of curriculum improvement involves a study of:
    a. the political, economic, and social structure of the surrounding society
    b. public opinion toward education
    c. advice or information for the public
    d. the aims and philosophy of current educational practice
    e. the abilities, needs, purposes and individual differences among the learners
    f. the origin and nature of subject matter
    g. the development of present curriculums
    h. the nature of modern outcomes of learning i. the many new techniques of evaluation
5. A program of curriculum improvement is far broader than the writing of a course of study or series of teachers' guides; it is concerned with the improvement of living and learning conditions in the school and in the community of which it is a part.
6. A program of curriculum improvement should result in changes of attitudes, appreciations, and skills on the part of the participants and in important changes in the learning situation.

C. CONDITIONS THAT COMPEL CURRICULAR CHANGES
1. Technological developments - In a society where most people work for someone else, it is important that the curriculum emphasize the attitudes and skills of cooperation.
2. International problems - The curriculum must emphasize international understanding as well as the defense of America and other freedom-loving nations.
3. Social change - The curriculum must prepare children for living in a complex and changing world, and must emphasize moral responsibility for one's acts both as an individual as well as a member of a group.
4. Educational progress - The increase of available materials of instruction and the expanding role of the teacher call for a redistribution of teachers' time and energies in terms of a new set of values.

D. CHANGES THAT RESULT FROM CURRICULUM IMPROVEMENT
1. In the professional staff-cooperative planning; working together on educational problems; experimentation with promising procedures; study of human growth and development.
2. In the teaching-learning situation - improvement in the school plant, equipment, and supplies; use of community resources; available community services; opportunities for children to participate in community life.
3. In improved pupil behavior - ability to define and solve meaningful problems: development of new interest; self-evaluation; skill in communication; skill in human relations; initiative; creative-ness .
4. In community relationships - participation by lay citizens; public support; public relations.
5. In school organization - plan of organization; staff selection procedures; school size; class size; daily schedules; district services; faculty conferences.

6. In instructional materials - cooperative production of instructional materials; more effective use of commercial materials; better selection of teaching aids; establishment of a "materials center"; development of a professional library.
7. In ways of working together - teacher-pupil planning; group dynamics; sociometric techniques; intergroup education.

E. MAIN PROBLEMS IN CURRICULUM DEVELOPMENT
1. The determination of educational directions
2. The selection of experiences comprising the educational program
3. The selection of a pattern of curriculum organization
4. The determination of principles and procedures by which the curriculum can be evaluated and changed

F. FACTORS AFFECTING CURRICULUM DEVELOPMENT
1. The existing political, economic, and social structure
2. Pressure exerted by minority groups or vested interests
3. Legislation
4. Tradition
5. Influence of logically organized subject matter and compartmen-talization
6. Textbooks

G. CONSIDERATIONS FOR CURRICULUM PROGRAMS
1. The improvement program is to be developed with the aid of supervisors, teachers, pupils, parents, and community.
2. The curriculum should be readily adaptable to individual differences, needs, and interests and to the special needs of groups, schools and communities.
3. There should be provision for articulation between and among the various divisions and levels of the school system.
4. There must be provision for continuous experimentation and research.
5. There must be flexibility and allowance for interpretation and change to meet new situations and conditions.
6. There must be provision for evaluation of principles, practices, and outcomes, as well as for appraisal of the curriculum improvement program itself.
7. The curriculum must provide conditions, situations, and activities favorable to the continuous growth and progress of each individual.
8. Curriculum policies and practices should encourage friendly understanding and democratic relations among supervisors, teachers, pupils and parents.
9. The success of a curriculum is dependent on competent leadership. (Supervision interprets and implements the curriculum and seeks to improve teaching and learning; teachers' attitudes and understandings determine the effectiveness of the curriculum; community aims, purposes, and resources exert an important influence on the curriculum; pupils help in developing a wholesome pattern of democratic living in which the curriculum operates most effectively.)

H. QUESTIONS RELATED TO CURRICULUM DEVELOPMENT
1. Why is the traditional curriculum, used with seeming success for years, now under such criticism, analysis, and change?
2. Is the curriculum an instrument of social progress?
3. Should the aims of education and the content of the curriculum be determined with some definiteness in advance of actual teaching-learning situations?
4. Is all, none, or a given part of the curriculum to be required of all learners - regardless of origin, present status, and very probable destiny?
5. How shall the curriculum be organized - scope and sequence determined?
6. How shall the curriculum content be selected?

7. What are the desired outcomes of learning experiences?
8. How much of the curriculum can be formulated by the pupils?
9. What stand shall the curriculum take on "indoctrination?"
10. What procedures should be used in reconstructing the curriculum?
11. What are the criteria for evaluating a curriculum?

III. GROUPING AND COMMITTEE WORK

A. ORGANIZING GROUPS FOR INSTRUCTION
   1. Know the children before you group
      a. General level of achievement (standardized tests)
      b. Individual problems in the area (everyday performance)
      c. Capacity to achieve (expectancy)
      d. Personal and social adjustment (sociogram)
   2. Develop a "readiness" for grouping
      a. Teach the techniques that will be the basis for independent activity later
      b. Be familiar with the types of exercises to be used for group work later; anticipate some of the skills which will be required
      c. Develop work-skills (choosing something, sharing materials, working independently, etc.)
   3. Launch the best group first
      a. The first group will be those children most advanced intellectually and socially
      b. The remainder of the class learns to work independently as the teacher works with the first group
      c. As both these groups learn to work simultaneously, the teacher notes the point at which further subdivision becomes necessary (for example, the slower group may be broken down into a normal and slow group)
   4. Group standards should be set cooperatively by the teacher and class
   5. Some abilities to aim for:
      a. Working alone
      b. Working quietly
      c. Completing a job
      d. Moving to the next job when the present one is completed
      e. Finding and correcting one's errors
      f. Evaluating one's own work
   6. Arrangement of pupils
      a. Reduce to a minimum the interference of one group with another (through location of groups in the room, allocation of blackboard space, etc.)
      b. Have a group's materials placed near to where that group works

B. CRITERIA FOR GROUP WORK
   1. Are the procedures used in accordance with the techniques advocated in the program of education?
      a. What is the basis on which the groups are set up? (Common weaknesses, sociogram, etc.)
      b. Is the goal for each group set and understood?
      c. Have these goals been set by cooperative planning?
      d. In what type of activity is the group engaged - individual or group? Is there a free interplay of minds at all times?

9

      e. Are there evidences of evaluation within the group - by individuals and by the group?
      f. What is the extent and variety of materials used?
  2. Are there evidences of individual contributions by children in the group?
  3. Are there evidences of committee work of children (charts, etc.)?
  4. Are there evidences of teacher-supervision of group procedures?
  5. Are there evidences of the growth of social skills, attitudes, and understandings of social living?

C. COMMITTEE WORK
  1. Group dynamics as a factor in committee work
      a. Sociograms and friendship charts
      b. Place of the "stars"
      c. Working the isolates into the committee
  2. As in grouping, the teacher starts with a single-committee and develops committee techniques with the members
  3. Selection of a chairman and a secretary by the committee -importance of leadership and followership
  4. Contributions of the members of a committee toward the solution of a problem - working together and all that it implies"
  5. Place of the teacher
      a. She never "abdicates her position;" she advises and guides when indicated
      b. She watches closely those members with personal problems
      c. She anticipates difficulties in human relations
      d. She assigns a place for the committee to work comfortably
      e. She displays charts listing the committees, with leaders starred
      f. She makes available materials for research, including pictorial material and special materials for the non-reader or retarded reader
      g. She checks the progress of the group and of the individuals in the group regularly (before a reporting period, etc.)
  6. Standards for group work periods

NOTE: These are suggestions for charts
    a. For a Group Leader
      a.1 Know what work to do each day
      a.2 Keep the group working
      a.3 Do not be too bossy
    b. For the Group
      b.1 We will speak softly
      b.2 We will talk only to our own group
      b.3 We will talk only about our own work
      b.4 We will try to find our own materials
      b.5 We will use our time wisely
      b.6 We will clean up when we have finished
    c. For Groups preparing a report
      c.1 Skim books for stories on the topic of your report
      c.2 Plan an outline of the whole topic
      c.3 Choose sub-topics for study
      c.4 Work on topics - make an outline, do some research, make something, etc.
      c.5 Give your report to the group for criticism c.6 Give the report to the class

IV. EVALUATION

A. ITEMS TO BE EVALUATED
1. Mental development *(traditionally, this has been almost the sole emphasis)*
2. Physical aspects
3. Social aspects
4. Emotional aspects

B. REASONS FOR EVALUATING
1. It is a means of discovering group and individual growth
2. It is a means of discovering whether children are developing at a rate commensurate with their general capacity (expectancy)
3. To discover children's strengths and weaknesses, and necessity for specific help (diagnostic) in particular cases
4. To indicate to the school how it can best provide the conditions of growth that make learning most economical and most effective
5. Children learn more effectively when they take part in evaluation
    a. As members of a group, they learn to become aware of group needs (through learning they must acquire for a specific purpose)
    b. They learn how to plan for group needs (through pratrtice in evaluating possible courses of action)
    c. They learn to take stock as they proceed with their tasks (through evaluating progress periodically)
    d. They learn ways of deciding when their project has reached a satisfactory conclusion (through practice in evaluating their achievements in the light of their original objectives)

C. WHEN TO EVALUATE
1. It is a continuing activity, taking place at every stage of the learning process *(Evaluation is not concerned solely with end products)*
2. The teacher evaluates situations as they occur
3. "The quality of living" that goes on in a classroom is evaluated as an indication of class morale
4. The amount of communication that takes place is, at all times, a significant evaluative factor
5. The need for recording social adjustments, emotional maturity, attention span, language development, interests, and enthusiasms of children makes continuous evaluation a necessity
6. Check lists and anecdotal records may be used to record what is observed

D. WHO EVALUATES?
1. Everyone concerned in the educative process should take part in evaluation
    a. The children, with or without the guidance of the teacher, make valid judgments
    b. The teacher evaluates herself, the effectiveness of her procedures, the progress of her class and the individuals therein, the climate of her room, and the classroom situation
    c. The school, as a composite of teachers and supervisors, evaluates its curriculum, its services to children, its growth of teachers and supervisors, and its relationship to the life of the community
    d. Members of the community, especially parents, evaluate the school, its program and its teachers (The school should provide such information so as to make possible an intelligent evaluation on the community's part)

E. EVALUATION IN A UNIT OF WORK
1. The unit should be evaluated in light of its objectives
2. The primary objective is not absorption of a mass of facts, but the development of attitudes, understandings, and appreciations
3. The evaluation of desirable social relationships, the development of good habits of work and thought, and the imparting of basic concepts are our major social studies goals
4. Measurement of the so-called intangibles, while admittedly difficult, is possible (Formal tests, such as the California Tests of Personality and Winnetka Behavior Rating Scale are not so valuable as teacher observation and judgment)
5. The teacher, by recording objectively significant behavior, can observe the developmental pattern of growth in chidren (anecdotal records, etc.)
6. Teacher-made checklists and tests are helpful in determining growth and progress
    a. Tests in ascertaining places where information is available (A test of this type may be administered before and after a unit is taken. Growth may be measured by comparing results)
        a.1 Whom would you ask where to find a certain building if you were downtown?
        a.2 How would you locate a certain book if you were in the library?
        a.3 If you weren't sure whether a word ended in "ant" or "ent," how could you find out?
        a.4 Where would you look to find out something about an explorer?
        a.5 How could you tell, by looking at a map, whether New York is closer to Connecticut than it is to Virginia?
    b. Tests involving the relevancy of data to particular problems and tests involving the relevancy of statements to a conclusion
        b.1 Does a person's race or religion have any bearing on his athletic or musical ability?
        b.2 Since your city uses great amounts of food, does that mean that your city produces huge amounts of meat, grain, etc.?
    c. Tests involving the reliability of various sources, the matching of persons with the fields of their probable competence
        c.1 Would Tiger Woods necessarily be an authority on international relations?
    d. Checklists of instances of voluntary cooperation (Does the child of his own accord clean up the area around his seat? Does the child bring materials from home?, etc.)
7. Methods of evaluation of a unit
    a. Objective tests *(prepared by teachers and pupils)*
    b. Teacher's written accounts and criticisms
    c. Teacher's anecdotal reports on individual and group work
    d. Matching achievement against predetermined objectives
    e. Comparison of activities and skills of this unit with those of preceding units
    f. Noting observations made by parents and community
8. Children's evaluation in a unit
    a. Charts: "Did I Do a Good Job?", etc.
    b. Evaluation "envelopes," in which children retain samples of their work and note-progress
    c. Children (and teacher) appraise:
        c.1 What have we learned?

c.2 What should we remember?
c.3 Did we do everything we set out to do?
c.4 What must still be done?
c.5 What could we have done better?
c.6 What questions should be included on a "test of all the important things we learned?"
c.7 How can we make further use of the things we learned?
9. Evaluation is a means of discovering:
   a. Group and individual growth
   b. Teacher-effectiveness or weakness
   c. Group needs
   d. Curriculum strengths or deficiencies
   e. Objectives realized
   f. Experience gained
   g. Subject matter acquired h. Skills mastered
   i. Evidences of creative expression
   j. Evidences of growth toward desirable habits, attitudes, and appreciations
   k. Activities not yet completed
   l. Subject matter not covered

V. DISCIPLINE

A. MEANING
   1. Broad Meaning - The attainment by the individual of such knowledges, skills, habits, and attitudes as will promote the well-being of himself and of his social group.
   2. Narrow Meaning - The creation of classroom conditions to provide a wholesome environment for the best functioning of the individual and the group.

B. DISCIPLINE VS. ORDER
   1. Difference
      a. Discipline: Based on self-direction; maintained by building habits of self-control and by stressing the social need for desirable conduct. It aims at a self-directed class that works quietly and efficiently even though the teacher is temporarily too busy to supervise the class.
      b. Order: Based on instant obedience to commands emanating from above; depends on the teacher's ability to exercise constant surveillance and to use the pupils' fear of detection as a deterrent to undesirable action. Order reaches its height when the teacher can make the meaningless boast that she "can hear a pin drop."
   2. As a means toward discipline, order is sometimes essential. It may be a legitimate aid to discipline. As a goal in itself, it has little justification.

C. THE DIFFERENCE BETWEEN CONDUCT AND BEHAVIOR
   1. Conduct: The adult's reaction to the child's acts. It is considered "good" or "bad." Depends on adult's standards or values.
   2. Behavior: The child's reaction to stimuli (physical, mental, or social). It is "normal" or "abnormal." Depends on child's personality.

D. PLANES OF DISCIPLINE
   1. Obedience - military concept
   2. Personal domination by the teacher - "good order" concept
   3. Social pressure - living and working with others

4. Self-discipline - living and working alone

E. GENERAL PRINCIPLES OF CLASSROOM DISCIPLINE
1. Self-control is achieved through proper habit formation (psychological principles)
2. Desirable discipline is social control within the school group
3. Discipline should be positive and constructive, rather than negative and destructive
4. It should appeal to the highest motives of which the pupil is capable
5. It should impress pupils as being fair, reasonable, and socially necessary

F. POSITIVE VS. NEGATIVE DISCIPLINE
1. The essential difference is one of attitude and approach
   a. Present conformity to rule vs. cultivating motives for sound action in later years
   b. Getting children to do the right thing vs. preventing them from doing the wrong thing

2. Examples:

POSITIVE	NEGATIVE
a. Stimulating attention.	a. Coping with inattention. Scolding.
b. Creating desire to come to school because of meaningful activities.	b. Devising measures to curb truancy. Scolding
c. Encouraging children to come early by starting promptly with interesting work and duties.	c. Devising new procedures to curb lateness. Scolding,
d. Awakening the desire to do things for the good of the to the school.	d. Compelling observance of class and school rules. Punishment.
e. Giving children opportunity of participating in class and school administration.	e. Teacher does everything, school. Doing things for children which they can be trained ties to do for themselves,

3. Caution: It is impossible to dispense with negative discipline entirely, but the emphasis should be placed on the positive plane.

G. WHY SOME TEACHERS HAVE DISCIPLINARY TROUBLES
1. Pedagogical Reasons
   a. Failure to employ appropriate subject matter and materials
   b. Poor teaching techniques
   c. Failure to consider the individual pupil's capacities, talents, and interests
2. Classroom Management
   a. Failure to mechanize routines
   b. Unattractive, physically uncomfortable surroundings
3. Personality
   a. Lack of tact
   b. High strung manner
   c. Idiosyncrasies in dress
   d. High pitched voice e. Lack of a sense of humor

4. Psychological
    a. Lack of sympathy with children
    b. Procrastination in handling cases (not facing the issue)
    c. Lack of a fair disciplinary policy

H. CLASS MORALE AS A FACTOR IN CLASSROOM DISCIPLINE
  1. Meaning of morale or class spirit
      a. "Morale is the feeling among members of a group that stimulates them to work happily together toward the realization of shared aims"
      b. "The personality of the group born of common attitudes"
  2. How Developed
  L a. *Leadership* of the teacher - she sets the tone
      a.1 Her personality - ability to fire others with enthusiasm for ideals and service; to arouse faith of pupils in her
      a.2 Her educational qualifications
      a.3 Her understanding of children
  A b. Stressing of strong social *attitudes* - work of the group more important than that of the individual - team work of pupils
  C c. Situations arousing *common* loyalties - participation in joint efforts
      c.1 Class projects - making things for the class or the school (posters, art objects, Christmas gifts to soldiers or destitute children, class newspaper, class party, help with parents' bazaar)
      c.2 Assembly programs, pageants
      c.3 Athletic teams
      c.4 Friendly competition with other classes (attendance records, contributions to the Red Cross)
  P d. Situations arousing *pride* as a result of achievement and recognition
      d.1 Service to the class and school
      d.2 Records - attendance, punctuality, neatness, cleanliness, etc.
      d.3 Good deeds and accomplishments of classmates
      d.4 Accomplishment of learning goals (New Program)
  S e. Attractive *surroundings* - contribution of pupils to the appearance of the room

                    (Mnemonic - S C A L P)

I. THE USE OF INCENTIVES
  1. Distinction between incentives and motives
      a. Incentive - An environmental object or condition, the attainment or avoidance of which motivates behavior (external) -praise, blame, reward, punishment, rivalry
      b. Motive - The process within an organism which energizes or directs it toward a specific line of behavior (internal) -interest, need, urge, drive, desire
      c. Incentive is the stimulus; motive is the reaction, though the terms, including "motivation," are used loosely and interchangeably.
  2. Real vs. Artificial Motivation (intrinsic vs. extrinsic)
      a. Real Motivation - Gives purpose and direction to the learning process, is part of the task, arises from the value of the task for its own sake, is related to the life of the child (aroused by problems or challenges to which the child desires the answer or solution)

      b.   Artificial Motivation - attempts to make uninteresting material attractive by sugarcoating; is based on traditional attitude that every lesson is a unit in itself; is usually unrelated or only slightly related to the task (stores, games, marks, rewards)

      c.   The new program vs. the traditional program from the point of view of motivation

      d.   Some examples of real and artificial motivation:

REAL	ARTIFICIAL
1. Arithmetic: Learning percents through computing class averages in attendance or the standing of athletic teams	1. Learning by reference to father's bank account
2. Spelling: Learning words by writing a real letter	2. Learning through the desire to get a better mark
3. Geography: Learning t?he geography of the city through trips and excursions	3. Learning in order to do well on a quiz
4. Science: Learning about plants through growing them	4. Learning through a reference to the flower shop around the corner or to a picture
5. Social Studies: Learning the industries of a country through a study of how people live and work	5. Learning through reference to the work children's "parents do
6. Art: Learning color and perspective through illustrating a unit by murals	6. Learning in order to get a good mark, to have work displayed, or to obtain the approval of the teacher

(NOTE: Extrinsic motivation is sometimes justifiable or desirable, but it should be subordinated to intrinsic drives wherever possible.)

    3.   Incentives in the Classroom
        a.   Principles
            a.1   The best incentive is one which makes a task significant to the child
            a.2   It should influence future as well as present actions and attitudes
            a.3   It should make doing an act a satisfying process
            a.4   It should encourage the social point of view
        b.   Motives to which the teacher can appeal
            b.1   The desire to do the right for its own sake should always be the ultimate goal even with very young children
            b.2   The desire for self-respect - knowledge of progress, recognition of abilities or status
            b.3   The desire to win the approval of one's fellow - displaying good work, posting lists of children doing well, monitorships
            b.4   The desire to gain the approval of the teacher or one's parents - praise succeeds better than blame, recognizing the good better than scolding the bad, letters to parents

- b.5 The desire for new experiences - problems, excursions, class clubs, projects
- b.6 The desire to win a reward - need not be of material value - praise, exhibition of work, monitorships should be within reach of all - avoid bribery

(NOTE: The lowest form of incentive is better than the best form of punishment.)

J. CLASSROOM PUNISHMENTS

1. The Basis for Punishment
    - a. What should be the aim? Retributive, deterrent, or corrective?
    - b. Punishment may be justified if it is *corrective*
        - b.1 It must be a means of removing a tendency to unsocial behavior
        - b.2 It must not be a separate entity, but part of the education process
        - b.3 It must aid in the process of adjusting behavior in a positive direction
    - c. Criteria of effective punishment
        - c.1 The child should be shown that he is being punished for a social transgression
        - c.2 The teacher's personal feelings must not be a consideration
        - c.3 Punishment is to be used only when the child fails to respond to intentives
        - c.4 It should be adapted to the child (not uniform)
        - c.5 It must not be unduly severe
        - c.6 It must not leave a residue of antagonism or resentment
        - c.7 It must not constitute the complete treatment for problem behavior
2. Punishment by Natural Consequence
    - a. It is sound in theory but difficult in practice in the classroom (copying, cheating, failing to do work, obscene language)
    - b. The principle can be followed, by making punishment seem to be a natural consequence wherever possible
3. Punishment by Fear
    - a. Fear is an inhibiting rather than a stimulating force. It has a paralyzing harmful effect on development. It should rarely be used
    - b. Corporal punishment is the lowest form of the use of fear. If ever administered, it should be for its shocking effect, rather than for punitive or corrective reasons
4. Evaluation of Classroom Punishments
    - a. Minor punishments, such as staring at a child or calling his name - effective in nipping trouble in the bud
    - b. Deprivation of position - effective if the door is held open for reinstatement
    - c. Reprimands - effective, if given unemotionally and child is shown how his act interferes with others (must be used sparingly)
    - d. Doing a written task - ineffective because it avoids the true causes of the trouble (I must come to school on time) and builds wrong associations (writing spelling words twenty five t imes)
    - e. Picking up papers, etc. - effective if used as a means of making up for an offense, doing a positive deed in place of a negative
    - f. Detention - generally ineffective because it leads to wrong associations with school

g. Isolation - of doubtful value. The practice of having a child stand in a corner or in the corridor has no justification
h. Social disapproval - effective if public humiliation does not result
i. Saturation - ineffective and dangerous (it may backfire)
j. Sarcasm - dangerous because mistaken for humor, builds resentment instead of cooperation (of doubtful value even with "smart alecks")
k. Epithets - unjustified
l. Sending for parent - effective if designed to understand causes and to devise program for cooperation between home and school

K. SOME PRACTICAL SUGGESTIONS FOR TEACHERS *(CHARACTERISTIC OF TRANSITION FROM ORDER TO DISCIPLINE)*
1. Give pupils the impression that you expect perfect order
2. Learn the names of all pupils as soon as possible
3. Give no unnecessary orders or directions - no repetitions
4. An explanatory statement, preparatory to giving a direction or order, reduces the possibility of confusion or disobedience
5. Insist upon a reasonable compliance with those directions which are given
6. Don't let little things go *(Nip disorder, in the bud)*
7. Keep the machinery of class management simple
8. Plan lessons and all work well
9. Keep the class busy on worthwhile work and activities
10. Use rewards and punishments judiciously - watch for and reward desirable actions
11. Avoid punishing in anger (It's the child, not the offense, that must be considered)
12. Don't punish the group for the offense of an individual
13. Don't make threats
14. Severe penalties should not be used for minor offenses
15. The teacher should never give the impression that she has exhausted her supply of punishments or rewards
16. Avoid forcing an issue with a disobedient pupil before the class
17. When a child is punished, keep the door open for him to return to the good graces of the class and the teacher
18. Have a sense of humor
19. Be fair and consistent in your decisions
20. Have an element of surprise - something new - in class work
21. Seat pupils so that opportunities for infraction are lessened
22. The voice should be subdued, but audible enough to be heard clearly throughout the room
23. Primarily, the handling of discipline cases is the responsibility of the teacher
24. In handling discipline cases, the teacher may have reasonable recourse to the parents
25. When a teacher has exhausted her own resources, or in the cases of emergency, she should call upon the supervisor for help

VI. BASIC FUNDAMENTALS OF EDUCATIONAL PSYCHOLOGY

A. CONDITIONING
Learning takes place as a result of experience with outside stimuli.
Responses are established by means of fixed associations.

1. Principles of Conditioning *(for use by teachers)*
   a. Learners' responses must be systematically studied
   b. Records of progress indicate need for change of pace, concentration on difficult parts, return to basic skills, new motivation, variations in use of cues
   c. Learner should make own records of progress
   d. Unlearning takes place rapidly; support and repeated reinforcement are required to consolidate and maintain habitual performance
   e. Teacher must control stimulating conditions (motivation)
   f. Teacher must help learner by providing varying conditions and extended practice
   g. Forced pacing methods are a poor substitute for adequate motivation

B. LEARNING BY TRIAL AND ERROR (CONNECTIONISM)

Learning involves the making of new mental and neural connections and the discarding or strengthening of old connections.

1. Concerned with what takes place between S-R to the neural connections
   a. Atomistic analysis of behavior
   b. Development is from hereditary instincts and reflexes to acquired habits
   c. Intellect and intelligence are quantitative
2. Thorndike's Laws of Learning
   a. Readiness - When a conduction unit is ready to act, conduction by it is satisfying and failure to conduct or being forced when not ready is annoying.
   b. Exercise - (Use and Disuse) Repetition with satisfaction strengthens the connection; disuse weakens the connection.
   c. Effect - Satisfaction strengthens the connection which it follows and to which it belongs. *(Importance of motivation)*
3. Thorndike's Five Characteristics of Learning
   a. Multiple responses to the same external situation pervade nine tenths of learning.
   b. The responses made are the product of the "set" or "attitude" of the learner. The satisfaction or annoyance produced by a response is conditioned by the learner's attitude.
   c. Partial Activity: One or another element in the situation may be prepotent in determining the response.
   d. Law of Assimilation or Analogy: If one element in the situation resembles another, it will call forth a corresponding response.
   e. Associative Shifting - Omitting elements of a situation and still getting the same response. *(Conditioned response)*
4. The Significance of "Cues" in Learning
   a. The learner tends to respond to loud sound, intense, brilliant or rapidly changing cues.
   b. Conspicuous stimuli may receive undue attention. Important stimuli may thus be overlooked.
   c. Cues help emphasize important stimuli.
   d. The teacher must discover when to use proper cues, and how much guidance to give the learner.

C. LEARNING BY INSIGHT: GESTALT PSYCHOLOGY
1. Constant striving to make sense out of a situation

2. The learner's efforts are not purely random
3. Understanding is enhanced by responding to total patterns, to relation between things
4. Motivation helps create perception of the problem
5. The learner's background of experience aids in insight, in perceiving figurations, in seeing the relationships of the parts to the whole, and in acquiring meaning and value

D. THE FIELD THEORY (ORGANISMIC, HOLISTIC THEORY)
   1. Derived from the Gestalt theory
   2. Insight is the alteration of organic structure within an area of the "whole organism"
   3. Significances
      a. Breakdown of atomistic views
      b. Importance of chemical function of neural mechanisms
      c. Fundamental role of "feelings and emotions" in learning
      d. Muscular coordination of the complete organism is a factor in skill acquisition
      e. Recognition of the principle of maturation
      f. Best motivation derives from needs of learners

E. TRANSFER OF TRAINING
   1. Recognized as significant in educational theory and practice
      a. Traditional Concept - Doctrine of Formal Discipline: the mind gains strength through use, and this strength is automatically available in all situations. (Faculties of the Mind)
      b. Current Concept - No faculties as such. Transfer is a fact of mental life occurring under certain mental conditions, not because of external causes.
   2. Factors Influencing Transfer
      a. Methods of procedure in learning and teaching
      b. Attitude of readiness set up by instructions given
      c. Degree of mastery of the material learned
      d. Integration of the initial learning - as to content and method
      e. Extent to which generalization and application are applied -"psychological organization"
   3. Current Theories of Transfer
      a. Theory of Identical Elements (Thorndike)
         a.1 Identity of content
         a.2 Identity of procedure
         a.3 Identity of aims or ideals
         These identical elements make use of the same neural bonds.
      b. Theory of Generalization or Abstraction or Relationship Transfer takes place to the extent that one generalizes his experiences and is able to apply general principles to different situations. (Scientific method)
   4. Implications for the Supervisor
      a. Materials used should have real value for children, not for mental discipline.
      b. A subject which has slight transfer value in a large field may be of more value than a subject which has a greater transfer value, but in a very limited field.
      c. The difficulty of a subject is not any indication of its transfer value.
      d. Recognition of child growth and development is the basic aim.

  e. The position accorded any subject in the school curriculum should be decided by the value of the special training it affords and by the social significance of its content rather than by its promise to develop general intellectual capacities.

5. Implications for the Teacher
  a. The most effective use of knowledge is assured, not through acquisition of any particular item of experience but only through the establishment of associations which give it general value.
  b. Transfer is most common at the higher levels of intellectual activity.
  c. Children should receive training in methods of memorizing, acquiring skills, and in solving problems.
  d. If transfer value is slight, then it is most economical to practice directly those habits and skills we wish to develop.
  e. An individual's ability to apply knowledge is not in proportion to his knowledge of facts.
  f. The teacher should know what it is that she wants the children to transfer to other fields, and she must learn by experience or experiment how to teach for transfer.
  g. The theory of transfer is recognized by all schools of psychology. More research is necessary before teachers can be guided by the theory to any great extent.

F. HABIT
1. Meaning - A learned response made automatically to the appropriate stimulus.
2. Principles of Habit Formation (Bagley)
  a. Focalize consciousness (Motivation)
    a.1 Give clearest possible idea of habit to be formed
    a.2 Use demonstration
    a.3 Make it vivid
    a.4 Arouse motivation .
    a.5 Give instruction in how habits are formed a.6 Multiple sense appeal
  b. Attentive repetition
    b.1 Vigorous, short, definite drill
    b.2 Use devices
    b.3 Have a definite goal (focalization)
    b.4 Watch for lag in attention
    b.5 Vary the number of repetitions
    b.6 "Practice makes perfect" only if with attention
  c. No exceptions
    c.1 Analyze habit in advance to prepare for likely slips
    c.2 Give special drill on difficult parts
    c.3 Put child on his guard c.4 Remove opposing stimuli
    c.5 Avoid forming similar habits at the same time
    c.6 Punishment, if necessary, should follow wrong act
  d. Automatization
    d.1 Attention to weak elements
    d.2 Distribution of practice (optional length)
3. Values and Limitations
  a. Diminishes fatigue because habit mechanizes reactions so that they accomplish their function with directness and minimum time and effort
  b. Releases consciousness for the guidance of other activities

c. Makes responses reliable and accurate
d. Complete domination, however, retards progress
e. Sensibilities often deadened, lessening normal emotional tones
f. Difficult to break bad habits
4. Breaking Bad Habits
   a. Avoid the situation which will result in the undesirable habit
   b. Avoid opportunity for its practice
   c. Concentrate on one or two bad habits at a time
   d. Follow the principles of habit formation for developing the reverse of the bad habit (Substitution)
   e. Attach unpleasant feeling tone
5. Significance for Teaching
   a. Dependence of habit on sensory stimulation *(Habits never initiate themselves)*
   b. Importance of gradation of subject matter to develop mechanical habits
   c. In skills, improvement is very rapid at first
   d. Attention to physical and psychical conditions (time of day, length of period, etc.)
   e. Recognition of possible periods of lapse and plateau
      e. 1 Need for rest
      e. 2 Attention and interest misdirected
      e. 3 Conflict in habits
      e. 4 Minor causes - indisposition, irritation
   f. Recognition of individual differences in habit formation
   g. Rate of forgetting high at first
   h. Consideration of Speed vs. Accuracy
   i. Recognition of three sets of habits (Mechanical; Subject Matter; Mental)

G. INDIVIDUAL DIFFERENCES
1. Principles
   a. Pupils differ in degree of ability, not in the ability itself
   b. Individuals differ in degree of difficulty of tasks which they can learn; also in the method of learning
   c. Pupils of the same age and grade differ greatly - there is considerable overlapping of successive grades
   d. No one class can ever be entirely homogeneous - variations are continuous
   e. There are no readily available and fixed categories which the school can employ for the purpose of differentiated instruction
   f. Provision for individualization presents teaching and administrative difficulties
   g. Chronological age alone cannot be the determinant of an individual's capacity
2. Conclusions for the School
   a. Administrative
      a. 1 Vary the time element
      a. 2 Flexible grouping
      a. 3 Testing programs
      a. 4 Modification of the curriculum
      a. 5 Provision for educational guidance
      a. 6 Flexible promotions

22

              a. 7   Supervision of proper teaching practices
      b.   Curricular
              b. 1   Individualization of instruction
              b. 2   Diagnostic testing and remedial teaching
              b. 3   Provision for individual methods of learning
              b. 4   Grouping within the class
              b. 5   Record of needs, progress, and evaluation

VII. HISTORY OF EDUCATION

A. LEADERS
1. Socrates (5th century B. C.)(469-399 B. C.)(Athens, Period of Sophists)
   - (1) Writings - Left no writings, is studied in works of Plato and Xenophon.
   - (2) Emphasis-Highest formulation of principles of moral life up to his time.
   - (3) Contributions - His starting point:"Man is the measure of all things" (Protagoras).
   - (4) Developed opinion into true or universal knowledge.
   - (5) Aid of education: Not sophist brilliancy of speech, but knowledge arising from power of thought, analysis of experience.
   - (6) Method: Dialectic, skillful questioning, distinguishing between permanent form and changing appearance, forming concepts from percepts.
2. Plato (4th century B.C.) (429-348 B.C.) (Athens, Academy)
   - (1) Writings - "Republic," "Dialogues."
   - (2) Three social classes: philosophers, warriors, workers.
   - (3) Six major concerns of life: psychology, knowledge, soul, state, politics, ethics.
   - (4) The ideal *State,* which exists for the realization of *justice,* consists of three classes of people: philosophers, soldiers, and workers.
   These classes of society correspond to the soul (or *psychology*) of the individual: intelligence or reason; the passions, spirit, or will; and the desires, appetites, or sensations.
   The *ethics of* the classes embraces the traits of character which they should exhibit: wisdom, or correctness of thought; honor, courage, energy of will, or justice of the heart; and temperance, self-control, or justice of the senses. *Politics* indicates the duties of the classes: the philosophers are to rule, the soldiers to protect and defend the State, and the workers to obey and support those above them.
   - (5) Aim of education: To discover and develop individual qualifications to fit into classes of society; harmony of individual and social motives.
3. Aristotle (3rd century B.C.) (384-322 B.C.)(Athens, Lyceum)
   - (1) Writings - "Organon," "Politics," "Ethics," "Metaphysics."
   - (2) Like Plato, he believed the highest art of man to be to direct society so as to produce the greatest good for mankind.
   - (3) Education is subject to politics, each kind of state having its appropriate kind of education.
   - (4) Education is a life activity.
   - (5) Method: Objective and scientific; used inductive method, and thus founded practically all the modern sciences.
   - (6) Education democratic, although all could not reach the same high point.
   - (7) Greatest systematizer of knowledge.

(8) Formulated deductive reasoning; dialectic given form and universal influence.
(9) Gave vocabulary of reasoning to the world.
4. Comenius (17th century)' (1592-1670)
    (1) Writings - "Orbus Pictus," "Vestibulum,""Janua,""School of Infancy," "The Great Didactic"
    (2) Sense - realist
        a. The teacher should appeal through sense-perception to understand the child
    (3) Contributions
        a. Forerunner of 18th and 19th century educational theory
        b. Reformed Latin textbooks
5. John Locke (17th century) (1632-1704)
    (1) Writings - "Essay on Conduct of the Human Understanding," "Thoughts"
    (2) Founder of modern psychology; advocate of faculty psychology
    (3) Empiricism; induction
    (4) Conception of the child's mind as a "tabula rasa" (blank slate)
    (5) His influence strong up to the middle of the 19th century
6. Rousseau (18th century) (1712-1778)
    (1) Writings - "La Nouvelle Heloise," "Emile"
    (2) Education is life, not preparation for life
    (3) Importance of the child
    (4) Functional education
    (5) Individual differences
7. Johann Bernard Basedow (18th century)(1723-1790)
    (1) Writings - "Elementarwerk," "Book of Method"; established school called Philanthropinum, at Dessau.
    (2) Belongs to the line of Sense-Realists following Eousseau and forerunner to Pestalozzi.
    (3) Made first attempt since Comeniums to improve the work of the school through the use of appropriate textbooks.
    (4) Ideas embodied:
        (a) Children to be treated as such, not as adults.
        (b) Each child taught a handicraft for educational and social reasons.
        (c) Vernacular rather than classical languages chief subject matter of education.
        (d) Instruction connected with realities rather than with words.
        (e) Rich and poor educated together.
    (5) Contributions
        (a) Trained teachers.
        (b) Milder form of discipline.
        (c) Broader and more philanthropic view of man's duty to his fellow-man.
8. Pestalozzi (18th and early 19th century)(1746-1827)
    (1) Writings - "How Gertrude Teaches Her Children/" "Leonard and Gertrude"
    (2) Sense impression
    (3) Respect for the individuality of the child
    (4) Discipline based upon love
    (5) Education for the subnormal
    (6) Normal schools

9. Herbart (19th and first half *of* the 19th century)(1776-1841)
    (1) Writings - First to write a textbook on psychology,"Testbook of Psychology"; Psychology as a Science"
    (2) Rejected the faculty psychology of Pestalozzi
    (3) Substituted his own method - the Five Formal Steps:
        (a) Preparation
        (b) Presentation
        (c) Comparison
        (d) Generalization
        (e) Application
    (4) Organization and technique of classroom instruction
    (5) Emphasis on environment in education
10. Froebel (first half of 19th century)(1782-1852)
    (1) Writings - "Education of Man," "Mutter," "Kose Lieder"
    (2) Founder of the kindergarten and the kindergarten idea
    (3) Education by doing
11. Spencer, Herbert (19th century) (1820-1903)
    (1) Writings - "Principles of Psychology," "Synthetic Philosophy," "Essays on Education"
    (2) Not originator but developer of the best in democratic education of his predecessors
    (3) Emphasis on scientific knowledge
12. Mann, Horace (19th century) (1796-1859)
    (1) Reference: Mary T.Mann, ed.,"The Life and Works of Horace Mann" (5 vols.-1891)
    (2) First secretary of the first Board of Education of Massachusetts (1817)
    (3) Conception of education as universal,secular,public,free, and compulsory
    (4) Outstanding organizer in education
13. Barnard, Henry (19th century) (1811-1900)
    (1) Writings - Edited "The American Journal of Education"(1855-1870)
    (2) Held positions in Connecticut and Rhode Island similar to that of Horace Mann in Massachusetts, i.e., Secretary of the Board of Education in Connecticut, 1838-1842, 1851-1855; and State Superintendent of Education in Rhode Island, 1845-1849.
    (3) First United States Commissioner of Education 1867-1870
14. Dewey, John (19th and 20th century) (1859-1952)
    (1) Writings - "The School and Society,""Democracy and Education," "Experience and Nature," "Freedom and Culture"
    (2) Education is life, not a preparation for life
    (3) Learning takes place by doing
    (4) The bases of education are psychological and sociological
    (5) Father of progressive education ("activity" program)

B. CONCEPTUALIZED DEFINITIONS AND AIMS OF EDUCATION
   1. Character, morality: Plutarch (Spartans), Herbart
   2. Perfect development: Plato,Rabelais,Montaigne,Comenius,Locke, Parker,Pestalozzi
   3. Happiness: Aristotle, James Mill
   4. Truth: Socrates
   5. Citizenship: Luther, Milton
   6. Mastery of nature: Bacon, Huxley

7. Religion: Comenius
8. Mental power, discipline: Locke, Van Dyke, Ruediger
9. Preparation for the future: Kant
10. Habits: Rousseau, William James
11. Unfolding: Froebel, Hegel
12. Holy life: Froebel
13. Interests: Herbart
14. Knowledge: L.F. Ward
15. Complete living: Spencer
16. Culture, liberal education: Dewey
17. Skill: Nathaniel Butler, E.G. Moore
18. Inheritance of culture: N.M. Butler
19. Socialization: W.T. Harris, Dewey
20. Social efficiency: Dewey, Bagley
21. Adjustment: Dewey, Ruediger, Chapman and Counts
22. Growth: Dewey
23. Organization of experience: Dewey
24. Self realization: Dewey and Tufts
25. Satisfying wants: Thorndike and Gates
26. Insight: Gentile